RAMAYANA

RAMAYANA

A Journey

Ranchor Prime

A CHANNEL FOUR BOOK

CONTENTS

Page 1: An eighteenth-century Rajasthan protrait of Lord Rama, the hero of Ramayana.

Pages 2–3: The army of monkeys and bears set out in pursuit of the demon-king Ravana.

Opposite: Sita and Rama enthroned, served by Hanuman, the divine monkey.

DEDICATION
To my spiritual master, Srila Prabhupada, who asked me to 'somehow or other preach about Krishna', and to my respected older god-brother Krishnadasa Swami, a dedicated servant of Lord Ramacandra, for his encouragement and advice.

INTRODUCTION

'I salute the sage Valmiki, who perches like a cuckoo on the tree of poetry, singing "Rama! Rama!" and who, though forever drinking from the ocean of the stories of Rama, is never sated.'

HE ORIGINAL RAMAYANA was composed in the distant past by the sage-poet Valmiki. Arranged into twenty-four thousand Sanskrit verses and divided into six books, this sacred scripture is a cornerstone of the Hindu, or more specifically the Vaishnava, faith. *Ramayana*, meaning 'Rama's travels', documents Rama's triumph over the demon-king Ravana, thereby enacting his fate as the ideal man and incarnation of the god Lord Vishnu. Memorized in full by Valmiki's disciples, *Ramayana* has been passed down through generations. From public readings to fireside retellings, this oral tradition is very much alive today; in India, there are famous reciters of *Ramayana* who know the whole story by heart.

The traditional way to appreciate *Ramayana* is to hear it in its entirety from beginning to end. Instructions are given for doing this in nine sittings, with breaks falling at the traditional places. This is still common practice at the great 'Rama Katha' festivals, which often attract tens, sometimes hundreds, of thousands of the faithful for the full nine days. The intention is to become so immersed in the stories of Rama that Rama, Sita and Hanuman come to life. This does not need to end with the recital; it can be a constant process of remembrance. By remembering Rama constantly one's whole life is sanctified, and the devotee comes to see Rama everywhere, as Sita did. This stage of life is described by Krishna: 'For one who sees Me everywhere and sees everything in Me, I am never lost, nor is he ever lost to Me.' (Bhagavad Gita 6.30)

In Indian villages it is customary to hear stories from *Ramayana* in the evening. After sunset villagers gather to hear the storyteller bring the characters to life; they cheer or cry as the story unfolds, then go home to sleep and dream of *Ramayana*.

Since the time of Valmiki, other poets have made their translations and adaptations of this epic, and *Ramayana* long ago migrated across south-east Asia to countries such as Thailand and Indonesia, each of whom have their own *Ramayana* literary traditions and have made it a part of their own culture. In Thailand, an officially Buddhist country, *Ramayana* dance-drama is the national dance, an inheritance of the country's ancient Hindu past, and the Thai king traditionally models himself on Rama. Indonesia, now predominantly Muslim, is famous for its shadow puppet theatre depicting *Ramayana*.

In India, *Ramayana* passed into each of the regional languages, such as Assamese, Bengali, Hindi, Kashmiri, Oriya, Kannada, Telugu and Malayalam, where it generated separate literary and religious traditions. Each region of the country has its own styles of *Ramayana* drama, such as the famous Kathakali dancers of Kerala, and elaborate dramatic productions are staged in the major cities. At festivals effigies of the demon-characters Ravana and Kumbhakarna are burned, or actors dressed as Sita and Rama are taken in procession. *Ramayana* is a staple of Indian cinema and the serialized *Ramayana* on television, broadcast for 78 weeks during 1987–88, brought the nation to a standstill for an hour each Sunday.

In all these ways, Rama has entered the subconscious of India. This is why, so long after its creation, *Ramayana* remains an essential part of Mother India, and the name of Rama echoes on a million lips every day, as it did on the lips of Mahatma Gandhi as he died.

Rama is God incarnate, the seventh incarnation of Vishnu. He chose to become human, and for the duration of his human life to forget his divine identity, or so it seemed. He suffered physical hardships and, when he lost his beloved Sita, a broken heart. On one level Rama's journey is an allegory for the journey every soul must make. In becoming human Rama shared in our human suffering and enacted the drama of our own lives – each of us endures our own banishment, our own loss, faces our own disillusions, and hopes eventually to learn acceptance of our lot and to find ultimate redemption. Thus to hear or to witness Rama's struggles is to relive our own lives, but in a divine context. Each episode in the story is multi-layered, working through individual karma, or destiny, and the divine lila, or play, of Rama. In the same way, India's present-day Vedic sages point to life itself as being the working out, for each of us, of our own personal web of karma, desires and free will in accordance or in conflict with the will of God.

THE WEB OF KARMA

One great theme of *Ramayana* is the working out of karma, the consequences of past deeds. The basic plot of *Ramayana* is a simple struggle between good and evil – the princess is kidnapped by the great evil one, then rescued by her lover and the evil one is vanquished; all live happily ever after. But it is not allowed to remain simple. We discover that there are many layers of karma involved and dilemmas to be faced, that the gap between good and evil is not as clear as we might have thought, and that behind this simple story lies a cosmic purpose to be fulfilled. At every step along the way we are tested emotionally and intellectually.

Rama's banishment is the first great hurdle. When his stepmother makes her extravagant demand for Rama to be exiled, we wonder why he should submit to such a spiteful scheme. Our sympathies go to Lakshmana, Rama's brother, who seems human in his intolerance and his chiding of Rama. But Rama insists it is his duty to do as he is asked, no matter how far-fetched that request may be. It is a matter of principle. What we don't know at this stage, but later realize, is that here there are greater forces at work. Dasaratha, Rama's father, has his own karma to answer to. When he was a young man he carelessly killed a youth and was cursed by the boy's father to die separated from his son. He had also unwisely pledged to Kaikeyi when he married her, in addition to her two wishes, that her son could be king. Unknown to us these consequences are being carried by Dasaratha, in exactly the way we might be carrying unknown consequences from our own past. Further, Rama's destiny as the incarnation of Vishnu requires him to leave Ayodhya for his eventual confrontation with Ravana. There is also the position of Sita. She had in a previous life, it is later revealed, sworn to bring about the downfall of Ravana, who had violated her chastity when she was incarnated as the divine ascetic Vedavati. In that previous birth she had performed penances to obtain Vishnu as her husband. All these factors come into play at the time of the banishment of Rama. Although it seems unjust, it is fated to happen, in order to fulfil a higher purpose.

In *Ramayana*, evil is ambiguous, and Ravana may not be as evil as he first appears. The story of Ravana's origin is told in another ancient Vedic literature, the *Srimad Bhagavatam*. Ravana was originally one of the gatekeepers of the spiritual realm of Vaikuntha, 'the place without suffering', where Vishnu has his eternal home. He mistakenly barred the exalted Kumara brothers from entering Vaikuntha and as a result was cursed to fall to the material world. He was given the choice between enduring three births as a demon or seven births as a godly being. In order to hasten his return he chose to be born three times as a demon and to be killed each time by Vishnu. In his first birth he was Hiranya Kasipu, who was killed by the fourth incarnation of Vishnu, Narasimha; in his second birth he was Ravana; and in his third birth he was to become Kamsa, the enemy of Krishna. His fight with Vishnu was therefore his way of assisting in the lila, or divine play, of Vishnu, and in this he was supported by Brahma, the creator. Ravana was born as the son of Visrava, grandson of Brahma, and gained great powers from Brahma which enabled him to terrorize the universe. With the help of his son Indrajit, also blessed by Brahma, he defeated his half-brother Kuvera, the treasurer of the gods, Indra the king of heaven and Yama the lord of death. Ravana's role as Vishnu's adversary explains why, at his funeral, Rama found some kind things to say about him.

Another paradox in *Ramayana* is the role of Vali. Vali is the enemy of Sugriva and an ally of Ravana. Yet he could hardly be called evil, particularly as he is the son of Indra, the king of heaven. Nevertheless Rama kills him. Vali misbehaved by banishing his brother and stealing his wife, but to punish him with death seems extreme. But once Rama has explained his reasons, Vali's anger dissipates and before he dies, instead of seeking to blame Rama for killing him, he begs Rama's forgiveness. Rama shows here that punishment can itself be an act of love. Putting this in the context of reincarnation, Rama explains that the karma of the criminal must be redeemed by accepting punishment if that karma is not to be carried forward to the next life, where it would bring further suffering. 'A sinner punished by the king is absolved and ascends to heaven,' declares *Ramayana*, and adds: 'A sinner released by the mercy of the king is also absolved, but the sin is transferred to the king.' In this context, Rama's killing of Vali is an act of mercy, and Rama is acting as the all-knowing God who dispenses justice with love.

FREEDOM AND DUTY

A central theme of *Ramayana* is the sacrifice of freedom for the sake of duty or honour. The Sanskrit word approximating 'duty' is dharma, which has no equivalent in English. Roughly translated, it means 'the essential purpose of life'. In Hindu society this manifests as a set of principles governing behaviour, such as the duty to obey one's father or to protect one's dependants. These principles governing the lives of the characters of *Ramayana* might seem oppressive in a modern context, yet on a higher level they embody a spirit of service that can be an expression of love. 'Love is as love does,' goes the saying. Love, if it is to be more than sentiment, demands service.

Hence Rama's devotion to Sita and his devotion for his people – both dharma – are in the higher sense an expression of love demanding the sacrifice of his personal freedom. This sacrifice of freedom is made not only by Rama, but by all the divine characters of *Ramayana*. 'When I was a child you took my hand and promised me your protection,' says Sita, 'and I have served you faithfully ever since.' Each exemplify the ideal of service in a particular relationship, Hanuman as a servant, Lakshmana as a friend and Sita as a lover. In the world of *Ramayana* there is no escaping dharma, which is each person's path to salvation. And when one duty appears to conflict with another, as when Rama's love for Sita conflicts with his duty to his people, Rama, and each one of us, is tested.

For many Hindus, Hanuman is the symbol of selfless service to God. It is no accident that a monkey should be accorded this honour: love transcends social standing or even race or species. When Jatayu, the faithful vulture who protects Sita, is killed by Ravana, Rama says of him, 'This king of birds was a great soul who sacrificed his life for my service. Souls such as this can be found everywhere, even among animals.'

If Rama, the incarnation of Vishnu and Lord of the Universe, is occupied in service, the same can be said of Krishna: 'There is no work prescribed for Me in the three planetary systems, and there is nothing I lack – yet I work. For if I should cease to work, these worlds would be destroyed.' (Bhagavad Gita 3.22–24) This is the vision of God given by the Vedic scriptures – a God who voluntarily serves his creation. In this spirit, Rama serves the demigods by killing Ravana, and he sets the example of an ideal king, who always serves his subjects. His rule is remembered in India as 'Ramaraja', and remains the ideal to which all rulers aspire.

THE IDEAL OF FOREST LIFE

The ever-present background to *Ramayana* is the forest. During Rama's long exile he and Sita visit the ashrams of sages, learning from them about spiritual life. The forest is never far away, and with it the ascetic life of the sages. It is said that these sages, who revered Rama as the incarnation of Vishnu and longed to be his devotees, were later born as the gopi cowherd girls of Vrindavan, when they were able to fulfil their desire by dancing in the forest with Lord Krishna. The beauty of the forest is woven throughout *Ramayana* in luxuriant passages of detailed imagery. But forest life is not easy, as Rama warns Sita at the outset; it represents the ideal of simple living and renunciation of the world which is the cornerstone of the Vedic spiritual path.

The forest could be interpreted as the womb from which all life emerges and into which all will return. Sita confesses her own fascination with the forest when she remembers the prediction made about her when she was a child: 'When I was a little girl a holy woman once came to our house,' she remembers, 'and I overheard her tell my mother that one day I would live in the forest. It is my destiny.' Hanuman is a resident of the forest, to which he returns at the end of the story, and indeed the story is written in the forest. This spirit of abandoning the world and returning to the simplicity of the forest beckons throughout. At the end of *Ramayana*, after Sita and Rama have regained the comforts of Ayodhya, it re-emerges when Sita asks to visit the ashrams, or hermitages, once more.

The final act of *Ramayana* is itself one of leaving. Rama and his entourage leave this world in its entirety. Perhaps this is Rama's profoundest message: this world is not to be enjoyed, although some pleasure may be found here. Ultimately the world does not allow itself to be enjoyed. We are all pitted against our own karma. Each of us carries into this world our own burden of karma from past lives. Our task while here is to assimilate this burden and come to terms with the lessons it has to teach. Only then can we turn our attention to finding our true purpose. The message is partly expressed by Vasistha when he advises Bharata after his father's funeral: 'Life and death, joy and sorrow, gain and loss: these dualities cannot be avoided. Learn to accept what you cannot change and give up sorrow.'

SITA'S SORROW

Valmiki prefaces *Ramayana* with the story of its making. He tells us how, in a state of grief and dismay, he composed a verse that gave expression to his emotion. This verse became the model for the entire epic poem of *Ramayana*, the thread that runs throughout it and which cannot be escaped: 'Hunter! Because you have so cruelly destroyed the happiness of these birds your happiness will also be destroyed!

Even Sita, mother of the world, is not exempt from sorrow. 'This body of mine was created only for sorrow,' she cries. 'What sin have I committed that I should be made to suffer like this?' Sita's suffering has been a source of perplexity to devotees for as long as *Ramayana* has been told. Why should Sita, the eternal companion of Vishnu, have to undergo such suffering? Some devotees accept the explanation offered in the *Kurma Purana*, where it is said that the original Sita was never taken by Ravana; a demon like him would be incapable of touching such a pure being. An illusory Sita was substituted for her, we are told, while the real Sita was sheltered by the Fire god. When the illusory Sita entered the fire after her rescue, the Fire god returned the original Sita to Rama unharmed.

But I prefer another approach. Sita's tribulations, in suffering separation from her lord, express the unconscious feelings of all souls separated from God in this world. To rediscover this inner sense of loss, of being separated from God, is the essence of the spiritual path of bhakti, devotion to God. The feeling of being abandoned by God, or of having abandoned God, is a recurrent theme in Vaishnava devotion. Far from taking them away from God, this emotion actually brings devotees closer to God through constant remembrance. When Hanuman first encountered Sita he found that 'She does not see the monsters surrounding her, or this heavenly garden, she sees only Rama.' This is the state of pure love, where none but the loved one is present in everything. This is why Hanuman begs Rama for the blessing to be able to remain in this world, even after Rama has departed, but to 'always be devoted to you and no one else,' and again why Lakshmana, in abandoning Sita, advises her to 'hold Rama always in your heart.' This spiritual union with the beloved in constant inner remembrance transcends physical union. It is the state of union with God which has been experienced by all the great devotional mystics.

I was first introduced to Lord Rama in my youth by my spiritual master, Srila Prabhupada, and take it as his grace that I have now received the chance to serve Rama by writing this new version of *Ramayana*. I chose for my source the original *Ramayana of Valmiki*, in the two-thousand page English edition of the Gita Press, first published in India in 1969. I am indebted to its translator, who out of modesty has remained anonymous. I have faithfully followed his verse-by-verse translation, in both pattern and content, while condensing it into modern English. I regularly used to hear the story of Rama or watch it enacted on stage, but when at last I turned to Valmiki's original text, in its English translation, I was overwhelmed by its beauty and depth, which brought many realizations welling up in my heart. I hope that by putting Valmiki's story into modern English, and making it accessible to a wider audience, I have helped others to taste something of the flavour of the original *Ramayana* and gain from it the inspiration I have found.

JAYA SITA RAMA

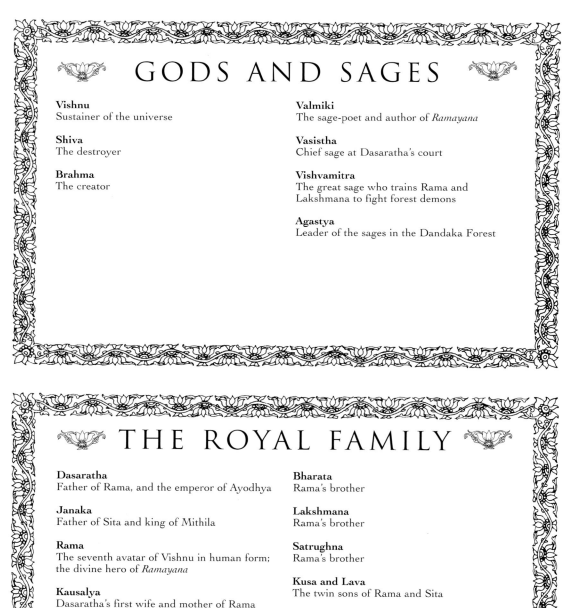

GODS AND SAGES

Vishnu
Sustainer of the universe

Shiva
The destroyer

Brahma
The creator

Valmiki
The sage-poet and author of *Ramayana*

Vasistha
Chief sage at Dasaratha's court

Vishvamitra
The great sage who trains Rama and
Lakshmana to fight forest demons

Agastya
Leader of the sages in the Dandaka Forest

THE ROYAL FAMILY

Dasaratha
Father of Rama, and the emperor of Ayodhya

Janaka
Father of Sita and king of Mithila

Rama
The seventh avatar of Vishnu in human form;
the divine hero of *Ramayana*

Kausalya
Dasaratha's first wife and mother of Rama

Kaikeyi
Dasaratha's youngest wife and mother of
Bharata

Sumitra
Dasaratha's middle wife and mother of twins
Lakshmana and Satrughna

Bharata
Rama's brother

Lakshmana
Rama's brother

Satrughna
Rama's brother

Kusa and Lava
The twin sons of Rama and Sita

Sita
The wife of Rama

Mandavi, Srutakirti and Urmila
Respective wives of Bharata, Satrughna and
Lakshmana

DEVAS AND ANIMAL LORDS

Indra
The Rain god, and king of heaven

Agni
The Fire god

Vayu
The Wind god, father of Hanuman

Varuna
God of the waters

Surya
The Sun god

Garuda
Lord of the birds, eagle-carrier of Vishnu

Hanuman
The monkey-servant of Rama and Sita

Jambavan
Lord of the bears and son of Brahma

Jatayu
The guardian of Sita and nephew of Garuda

Vali
The monkey brother of Sugriva

Sugriva
The outcast younger monkey-brother of Vali

Angada
The son of Vali

THE RAKSHASAS OF LANKA

Ravana
The king of the demon gods

Dusana
The cousin of the demon-king Ravana

Indrajit
Ravana's eldest son

Khara
The cousin of Ravana

Kumbhakarna
Brother of Ravana

Mandodari
Ravana's queen, and mother of Indrajit

Maricha
The magician uncle of Ravana

Surpanakha
A demoness, sister of Ravana

Tataka
A man-eating demoness

Vibhisana
Brother of Ravana who fights with Rama

Suka
Ravana's spy

PROLOGUE

Let me tell you how this story came to be told. Long ago the sage Valmiki lived with his disciples beside the river Tamasa in the forests of Northern India. They lived a life of prayer and meditation in simple huts woven from branches, leaves and grass. Early one morning the great Narada, who can fly at will through the sky to visit any planet in the universe, appeared before Valmiki who greeted him with reverence and offered him a seat. In the presence of this great personality Valmiki asked a long-cherished question: 'Tell me, Narada, who is the greatest person in the world? Who is accomplished, learned, powerful, beautiful, truthful, and cares for all creatures? Who is without anger, yet sends fear into the hearts of enemies?'

Narada smiled as he replied: 'The person you seek is extremely hard to find among ordinary mortals. There is, however, a famous king by the name of Rama. He is strong and beautiful, wise and compassionate, pure in character and loved by all. He has deeply studied the ancient wisdom, is brilliant in archery and courageous in battle. In gravity he is like the ocean, in constancy like the Himalayas and in generosity like rain. Let me tell you about Rama: how he was forced to give up his throne and live in the forest, how he rescued his wife Sita from the evil Ravana and how he returned to rule his people with justice and love.'

Valmiki sat in rapt attention as Narada recounted the wonderful story of Rama. At last he fell silent, saying, 'Whoever hears the noble story of Rama's deeds will be blessed with success in this life, and peace in the next.' Valmiki bowed low in gratitude as Narada left, disappearing into the sky as the sun passes behind a cloud.

Valmiki called his disciple Bharadvaja to accompany him to the river for his noon bath and meditation. Here, Valmiki noticed a pair of cranes joyfully sporting and singing. As he watched the birds, a hunter sprang from the forest and shot an arrow through the heart of the male. The stricken bird fluttered to the ground and breathed his last, and his mate wailed pitifully. Valmiki was filled with pain to see such cruelty.

'Hunter! Because you have so cruelly destroyed the happiness of these birds your happiness will also be destroyed!'

No sooner had the words left his mouth than he stopped in surprise. He repeated the words again to himself and then spoke them out loud to Bharadvaja, saying: 'These words of grief and dismay have emerged in the form of a verse, with four feet of eight letters each, which can be sung with a lute.'

As Valmiki returned to his cottage, singing the verse to himself, he saw that he had another visitor, even more illustrious than the first. It was Lord Brahma, the creator of the universe and father of Narada. Again with respect Valmiki greeted his guest and offered him a seat. As Brahma made himself comfortable, he heard Valmiki quietly singing to himself his new-found verse.

'Ah!' he said, 'you have created a verse expressing your grief. It was me who inspired you to do this. The time has come for you to write the sacred and soul-stirring song of the lives of Sita and Rama as you have heard it from Narada. As you do so, all its details will be revealed to you through divine inspiration. Use this style of verse and your song will be remembered as long as the mountains and seas remain.' Then Lord Brahma left, and Valmiki and his disciples continued to sing the verse in wonder, and the more they sang, the more their wonder grew.

The next day, Valmiki withdrew to a silent and undisturbed place and sat facing east to absorb himself in meditation. Entering a deep trance he saw in his mind's eye the figures of Rama and Sita. He saw Rama's father Dasaratha, with his queens surrounding him, all laughing and talking. Then he saw Rama roaming in the forest in the company of Sita and Lakshmana. Gradually the whole tale of Rama and Sita unfolded before him in exquisite detail. At last he stirred from his trance.

Then Valmiki composed the story as an epic poem. He divided it into six cantos and taught it to his disciples, Kusa and Lava. They travelled the country reciting the story and their fame spread, until one day they arrived in the city of Ayodhya and were brought before King Rama himself. Rama, his three brothers, ministers and courtiers sat silently as the boys began to sing. Kusa and Lava lifted their sweet voices in clear notes, and here follows their sacred tale called *Ramayana* – the Journey of Rama.

The sage-poet Valmiki teaches Ramayana *in Dandaka Forest.*
His disciples, Kusa and Lava, listen attentively.

THE FIRST BOOK

Bala Kanda

Emperor Dasaratha worships the gods to get a son, and as a result received four divine sons as incarnations of the god Vishnu. The picture shows the king, aided by his royal priest Vasistha, presiding over a ceremony to bless his newly-born sons, Rama, Bharata, Lakshmana and Satrughna, held in the arms of their mothers, Kausalya, Kaikeyi and Sumitra. Meanwhile Sumantra, the king's minister, reads from the hymns of the Vedas and in the foreground priests pour grains and ghee into the sacred fire.

RAMA'S YOUTH

DIVINE BIRTH

HERE WAS ONCE A prosperous kingdom called Koshala on the banks of the river Sarayu. At its heart lay the vast and fabulous city of Ayodhya, laid out in broad avenues with exquisite gardens and cool mango groves. Its streets were thronged with foreign princes and beautiful women; its market places were always full to overflowing and poverty and crime were unheard of. The scholars of Ayodhya were deeply learned in the Vedic wisdom and it had many palaces and seven-storey buildings. All was surrounded by a deep moat defended by powerful warriors expert in the mystic arts of Vedic archery, and was impregnable to invaders.

Emperor Dasaratha, the ruler of Koshala, was a great and powerful hero descended from the mighty Iksvaku race. He was devoted to truth and much beloved by the people of Koshala. He was advised by learned sages headed by the famous Vasistha and assisted by eight ministers, chief of whom was Sumantra. These men were wise, good-natured and truthful and acted only for the benefit of the whole population. The emperor was an expert statesman with many allies. Under his astute rule Ayodhya became so wealthy that it vied with the wealth of Indra, the king of heaven.

However, despite all his wealth, the emperor was not happy because he did not have a child. He had ruled for thousands of years and had grown tired, but still he had no heir. One day he decided to take action: he would stage the ultimate royal ceremony called asvamedha, or the horse sacrifice. Such a ritual could be undertaken only by a king of unsurpassed power, but if done according to the Vedic codes with the proper Sanskrit invocations it could produce magical results and fulfil any desire. To be sure of success it was necessary to have an exalted priest in charge of the sacrifice, so the emperor sent for Rishyasringa, a fabled youth who, it was foretold, had been destined specially for this task.

Elaborate preparations began. The most important part of the sacrifice was the horse himself. This could be no ordinary horse but was to be the most beautiful and noble stallion the emperor possessed. At the conclusion of the ritual the horse would lose his life, but in so doing would be reborn into the heavenly kingdom. While the ground was prepared for the great sacrifice, the horse was released to roam freely, accompanied by a royal guard, and wherever he went he received tribute. After one year had passed he was brought back and a huge assembly gathered in tents and pavilions outside the city. In that assembly were kings and queens, princes and princesses, and nobles from far-off lands, all of whom brought costly gifts. For three days mystic hymns were chanted and eighteen sacred fires burned. At each step in the proceedings, mantras were chanted with the proper pronunciation and melodies. These mantras, chanted by the exalted Rishyasringa, summoned the gods themselves from heaven to witness the sacrifice.

Unseen by the ordinary people, the gods gathered at the sacrifice around the venerable Lord Brahma, creator of the universe, and spoke to him urgently: 'The demon-king Ravana is terrorizing us all. Because of the boons you gave him he has become invincible and is threatening to overthrow Indra, the king of heaven. Already he has stolen Kuvera's aerial chariot and has killed many amongst us, yet he seems to gain more strength each day. Please find a way to rid us of him.'

'I did grant Ravana invincibility from the attack of any kind of god or heavenly being,' confirmed Brahma, 'but at the time he made no mention of human beings, whom he thought insignificant. Therefore only a human being can kill him.'

The gods were delighted to learn this secret and considered how to act upon it. While they were deep in thought the mighty Lord Vishnu appeared in their midst and took his seat next to Brahma. He was dressed in yellow and shone like the sun, radiating peace and tranquillity.

'O Lord of the Universe,' petitioned the gods, 'please save us from Ravana by

The elaborately decorated sacrificial horse is released by the priest Rishyasringa, to roam
for a year in preparation for the asvamedha sacrifice of Emperor Dasaratha.

entering the world of humans as the four sons of the noble Emperor Dasaratha. In those human forms you can challenge Ravana, who takes pleasure in killing the innocent and terrorizing the whole universe. Please put an end to him.'

'Have no fear,' said Vishnu. 'As Rama I will fight in human form with the terrible Ravana and kill him and his entire race. I will then rule on earth for eleven thousand years to re-establish peace and prosperity.' Saying this Vishnu, ever ready to serve his devotees, thought of Ayodhya as his home and Dasaratha as his father and vanished from the sight of the gods.

Emperor Dasaratha and his attendants, unaware of what had taken place on the higher plane, brought the horse to be sacrificed according to the ancient rite, by which it was awarded a new life. When all this was completed, a brilliant red-robed figure, of awesome size, but who had gentle features, appeared from the sacrificial fire. Cradled in his arms was a golden bowl with a silver lid.

'I am a messenger of Vishnu who has come to congratulate Emperor Dasaratha on the success of his sacrifice. In this bowl is magical food. When the emperor feeds it to his queens, they will bear him four sons according to his wish.' The wonderful figure gave the bowl to the emperor and melted back into the fire.

Dasaratha hurried off to his queens in their private apartments. He gave half the bowl's contents to Queen Kausalya, his first wife, a third of what remained to Kaikeyi, the youngest, and the rest to Sumitra, his middle wife. In the course of time all three wives became pregnant and their beauty grew, as if they carried inside them the sun and the stars.

Meanwhile Lord Brahma gathered around him the inner circle of gods and issued some instructions: 'Now that Vishnu is to be born as the sons of Dasaratha, he will need help to overthrow Ravana. You will need to create a race of divine monkeys with powers equal to yourselves. They must change their shapes at will, and perform supernatural feats to destroy any opponent in battle.'

Being so commanded the gods created monkey-sons in the image of themselves. Indra the king of heaven had Vali, who became the monkey-king. Vali's brother was Sugriva, born to Surya the Sun god. Others were born to each of the gods, and the strongest and wisest of them all was the glorious Hanuman, son of Vayu the Wind god, whose body was as strong as a thunderbolt and as swift as the wind. So came into being within a short time a race of giant monkeys who lived in the jungles eating only fruit but whose strength and power had no limit. Roaming about the forests they played havoc, uprooting trees and catching hold of maddened elephants at will. Ten million of them gathered

A messenger of the god Vishnu steps from the sacrificial fire to present magical food for Dasaratha's queens. Vishnu is re-born, in human form, as their sons.

The young prince Rama, with his three brothers, learns the skills of warfare and sporting as part of his education, which also included politics, economics, the arts and the holy scriptures.

around their two leaders, Vali and Sugriva, like a mass of clouds around two mountain peaks, ready to serve Lord Rama when he would call on them.

In the spring of the following year, on the ninth day of the new moon of Chaitra, the planets were exalted in the heavens. The glorious moment had arrived for the birth of Lord Rama to the happy Queen Kausalya. The child embodied half of Lord Vishnu and was marked with signs of divinity such as reddish eyes and long arms. On the next day Bharata was born to the youngest queen, Kaikeyi, and Queen Sumitra gave birth to twins, Lakshmana and Satrughna, all of whom were one-sixth part of Vishnu.

When the news reached the people of Ayodhya they danced and sang in the streets. The emperor opened his treasure house and gave gifts to the musicians and priests. Showers of petals fell from the skies and everyone rejoiced.

THE DEVAS

Brahma, the creator of the universe, is depicted here with five heads rather than the usual four. He rides on his swan-carrier and holds the hymns of the Vedas.

BRAHMA is born from a lotus flower from the navel of Vishnu, the Lord of the Universe. Brahma creates thousands of gods, or devas, who are put in charge of the cosmic order. Indra governs the rain, Vayu governs the wind, Agni fire, Surya the sun, Chandra the moon, Varuna the waters and Goddess Bhumi the earth. Yama, the god of death, is given charge of the law of karma (see page 52).

In Hinduism, Brahma and the devas are thought to create the myriad lifeforms of the universe, among them human beings. The devas have the power to grant blessings to their worshippers. For devout Hindus these devas are not mythical figures; they are the powers behind the elements of the natural world such as wind, rain and the earth itself. However, powerful though the devas are, behind them lies Vishnu:

'When people desire to worship the devas, I make their faith steady so they can devote themselves to their chosen deity. Endowed with firm faith, they obtain their desires, but these benefits are bestowed by Me alone.'

BHAGAVAD GITA 7.21–22

With the passing of the years the boys excelled in their studies and grew tall, strong and virtuous. Lakshmana served Rama and Satrughna served Bharata. Lakshmana would not eat until Rama had eaten, or sleep without him. Whenever Rama went to the forest Lakshmana loved to follow, protecting him from all harm. Rama was deeply loved by the people and was always the one apart, like the full moon in a clear sky.

TRIAL OF COURAGE

The princes' education was nearly complete and the emperor began to think about getting them married. One day, as he was discussing this with his counsellors, the great sage Vishvamitra arrived at the palace gate, burning with brilliance from all the penances he had made. The emperor personally came out to greet him, offering him water to wash his hands as was the custom.

'I hope all goes well in your kingdom,' said the sage, 'and that you are faithfully carrying out your duties as emperor.' Dasaratha happily brought his visitor inside and together they entered the court.

'Your arrival is like rain on a parched land or sunrise after a long night. Today my life is complete. Please tell me how I may serve you. Whatever you ask will be done.' Encouraged by Dasaratha's generous words, the sage then responded:

'Oh, tiger among kings! I have undertaken an important sacrifice at my ashram, but whenever I get near the end two demons of the night sent by the demon-king Ravana pollute my altar with flesh and blood, spoiling everything. Ravana is the sworn enemy of all sages and is terrorizing the whole universe. These helpers of his are extremely powerful. Please give me your eldest son, Rama, for just ten days. Although he is young he has divine powers and he is the only one who can destroy demons. In return I shall teach him the secrets of many powerful weapons possessed only by me.'

When the emperor heard Vishvamitra's request he became very distressed and said:

'My beloved Rama is only sixteen and has not finished his education. He is no match for such treacherous demons. Even I cannot face the might of Ravana. Nevertheless, take me instead. I will personally stand guard over your sacrifice with my army. I am prepared to risk my life to help you, but not the life of my boy.'

These words fell on the sage's ears like oil on fire, and he began to tremble with rage so that the very ground shook beneath his feet. Vasistha, the emperor's personal adviser, quickly stepped forward.

'Do not refuse his request, my lord, or his anger will destroy us all. There is no need to worry about Rama's safety. Vishvamitra, who knows the secrets of mystic combat, will protect him. This is a rare opportunity for the princes to learn the secrets of warfare that he alone knows. His coming is a blessing.'

Hearing these words the emperor relented. He called for Rama and Lakshmana and blessed them before handing them over to Vishvamitra, instructing them to look upon

The demoness Tataka casts magical dust during Rama and Lakshmana's initiation into physical and spiritual battle. The brothers are protected by mantras, making them invincible.

the sage as their father and do whatever he asked. Satisfied, Vishvamitra turned and left with the two boys behind him. As they walked out of the court a cool breeze blew, flowers fell from the heavens and celestial drums sounded.

Before long they had left the city of Ayodhya far behind. Vishvamitra led the way, following the course of the River Sarayu. They walked quickly, the princes carrying their bows and quivers full of arrows. After some time they came to a sheltered spot where they halted at the water's edge.

'Before going any further I want to initiate you both with mantras to protect you from hunger and thirst and give you unlimited strength,' said Vishvamitra. 'Armed with these mantras you will be invincible even when you are asleep.'

He told them to sip water from the river and repeat after him the mantras called Bala and Atibala, which they soon learned by heart. When he had received his mantra, Rama began to glow like the autumn sun.

They stayed there for the night, sleeping on the bare ground. The royal princes had never slept anywhere but in the safety and comfort of their beds, but soothed by Vishvamitra's words they drifted peacefully to sleep beneath the glittering stars.

Before dawn, Vishvamitra woke the two boys and made them bathe and perform morning meditation in honour of the Sun god. After eating a meal of fruits and berries, they set off again, marching west. All day they walked until they reached the confluence of the Sarayu and the mighty Ganges. Here, on the headland between the two rivers, lived a colony of forest sages. Through psychic vision, they had long been aware of the strangers' approach. They honoured the great Vishvamitra with respectful words and made the travellers comfortable for the night in simple dwellings. Hearing of their purpose to rid the region of the terrors of Ravana's demons they wished them god-speed, and the following morning helped them across the swift-flowing waters of the Ganges.

Their way forward then lay through dark and tangled jungles infested by fierce animals and echoing with the cries of strange birds. All day they walked, deeper and deeper into the forest.

'What is this fearful place?' asked Rama. 'It is full of lions, tigers and elephants but I see no sign of any humans. It feels as if there is something terrible here that has frightened them away.'

'This was once a fertile and prosperous land,' Vishvamitra told them, 'but it has fallen under the sway of the man-eating demoness Tataka, who is the mother of the demons who are troubling my sacrifice. She has the strength of a thousand elephants and no one can withstand her.' Vishvamitra then revealed that he had brought them to this place to test them against the demoness Tataka.

'She is female,' he said, 'and ought not to be harmed, but it is your duty to protect the innocent from her. You have no alternative but to kill her. That is my order.'

'You are now my guru and I have sworn to obey your orders,' replied Rama. 'I will do as you ask.'

As they talked they reached a clearing in the trees. Rama halted and raised his bow. He drew the string and released it with a deep ring that resounded through the forest. It penetrated Tataka's cave and stunned her, pulsing through her like a wave of agony. Enraged at this intrusion into her kingdom she rose up and flew over the treetops searching for its source. In no time she came upon Rama and Lakshmana in the clearing. Keeping her distance she circled them from above, not knowing who these bright and terrible beings were. Rama saw her ugly and deformed shape and felt pity for this loathsome creature. He turned to Lakshmana and said to him:

'She is a woman, Lakshmana, and I have no desire to kill her, evil though she may be. I will punish her by cutting off her nose and ears and then allow her to escape with her life.' But even as he spoke Tataka discharged a magical cloud of dust hiding her from view, and from behind this she began to bombard Rama and Lakshmana with volleys of rocks and boulders. Aiming by sound alone, Rama struck her with razor-sharp arrows that sliced off her arms, and Lakshmana sent arrows that cut off her nose and ears. Still she did not retreat. Assuming another shape Tataka renewed her attack on the princes, throwing rocks from all sides at once.

'Do not play with this dangerous creature,' warned Vishvamitra. 'Dusk is approaching and with the darkness her strength will increase. Kill her now!'

Rama saw her rushing headlong towards him through the growing darkness. Quick as lightning he met her with a shaft from his bow as powerful as a thunderbolt, penetrating deep into her heart. She let out a piercing scream and fell dead.

Peace descended upon the forest and, released from Tataka's deadly spells, the place seemed to shine in the darkness. Exhausted, the princes decided to rest for the night in that very spot.

The following morning Vishvamitra decided it was time to reward his courageous disciple, Rama, with the divine weapons that he had in his possession. No ordinary weapons, these took the outward form of arrows, javelins or discs, but were controlled by mantras and endowed with inconceivable potencies. They were cosmic spells, capable of destroying the most powerful enemy, or even entire armies.

There in the forest clearing Vishvamitra taught Rama the invocations and mantras to release and recall a hundred divine weapons, one by one. Each weapon belonged to a particular deity and had its own etheric form. As the magic spells were uttered the forest glade filled up with their shadowy presences, until a host of mysterious beings surrounded Rama. Some glowed like coals, some smoked, some were brilliant as the sun and some were cool like the moon. Together they bowed before Rama and offered him their services.

'For the time being I have no need of you,' Rama said, 'but when danger threatens, please at once enter my mind.' Silently, they walked around him in respect and faded into the shadows.

Continuing on their way they walked all day until, emerging from the dense forest, they saw before them a mountain on whose side clustered a beautiful grove of trees like a cloud. This was Siddha Ashram, the hermitage of Vishvamitra. It was a deeply sanctified place, having once belonged to Vishnu in his incarnation of Vamana.

'This place belongs to Vishnu and has the power to end a person's cycle of rebirth. Please consider it your own, Rama, as I know you to be Vishnu in human form.' On saying this, Vishvamitra led the boys by the hand into the grove. As they entered, disciples emerged from the trees on all sides to pay their respects to their guru and welcome the two princes. They were fed on simple forest fare and given a place to rest. Meanwhile, as night fell, Vishvamitra started to prepare for the great sacrifice, consecrating the altar and sanctifying himself through chanting Vedic hymns. From that moment he observed a vow of silence.

The boys rose early the next day. They observed their morning meditation and then prepared themselves for action.

'When will the demons of the night come, and from what direction?' they asked.

'The attack will come from the sky from any direction and at any time without warning,' they were told. 'For the next six days you must be constantly on your guard, day and night.'

They stationed themselves with their bows beside the altar of sacrifice and kept watch continuously for five days and nights without incident. By the time night fell on the sixth day still there was no sign of the assailants. As midnight approached the sacrifice neared its climax and a chill fell on the night air. Suddenly the flames of the sacred fire leaped high. In the distance, faintly at first, they heard a series of blood-curdling shrieks approaching rapidly in their direction. Two dark and terrible shapes hurtled out of the sky and swooped low over the altar, raining blood and lumps of flesh in all directions and spreading a foul and stifling odour. They seemed to hesitate in their onward flight, sensing the presence of the two young defenders. In a moment they were back.

By the flickering light of the fire Rama saw them coming straight at him. Keeping his nerve he called for Sitesu, the weapon of Manu, which repels opponents like a hurricane ripping through clouds, and discharged it at the leading demon. Its effect was instantaneous. It struck the demon full on the chest and hurled him with such force that it propelled him hundreds of miles out across the Indian ocean. Next Rama summoned Sikhara, the weapon of the Fire god, and aimed it at the second demon. It pierced him in the heart and killed him instantly. That night there was great rejoicing in Siddha Ashram and everyone hailed the princes as heroes.

Rama and Lakshmana asked Vishvamitra what he now wanted them to do. He told them about a great sacrifice that was to take place at the court of King Janaka in Mithila, several days' journey to the north. 'King Janaka possesses a miraculous bow, that once belonged to Lord Shiva,' he told them. 'This bow is so mighty that neither man nor god can even lift it. He keeps it in his court and worships it with incense and offerings. I am to assist a great sacrifice that Janaka is organizing. You two come with me and I will show you the bow.'

Next morning they set off with their guru, accompanied by a host of his followers. As they journeyed along the banks of the Ganges he told them many stories from the history of those parts. Each evening they sat up late into the night listening to him with fascination. One night he narrated the sacred history of the descent of the Ganges. He told them how she was born as Ganga, daughter of the Himalayas; how she was taken up to heaven as the celestial Milky Way; how she was brought to earth by the penances of King Bhagiratha and caught in Lord Shiva's hair; how she thundered through mountain ravines on her way to the plains; how she washed away sins; and finally how she entered the underworld. As Vishvamitra spoke, the night deepened.

'Come,' he said, 'the forest is wrapped in silence and the trees are still. The moon is rising and spreading its soothing rays. The firmament is thick with stars like jewelled eyes. Birds and beasts are buried in slumber while nocturnal creatures and demons roam the darkness. Half the night is passed and we have far to go. Let us sleep.'

FATEFUL LOVE

Outside the city of Mithila there was a great commotion. An enormous festival ground was being prepared for King Janaka's sacrifice, which would last twelve days. Hundreds of tents had been erected and enclosures set apart for groups of rishis coming from all over India.

Vishvamitra's party, with Rama and Lakshmana, set up camp. News of their arrival was carried to King Janaka, who hastened out to greet the sage. Vishvamitra introduced the two princes as the sons of Dasaratha and told Janaka of their extraordinary exploits. When he saw them he was quite astonished by their beauty and strength; to him they looked like living gods. Then Vishvamitra asked Janaka to show them the great bow.

'This bow originally belonged to Lord Shiva,' explained Janaka, 'but he gave it to my ancestor Devavrata and it has stayed here ever since. No one has ever been able to lift it – let alone string it – although many have tried.'

Now it so happened that Janaka had a beautiful daughter, miraculously born from the earth. Her name was Sita, which means 'furrow', because she appeared out of the earth from a furrow ploughed by the king when he was levelling the ground for a great sacrifice. The king had adopted her as his daughter and loved her dearly. She was so famous for her beauty that Mithila had once been besieged by kings fighting to win her hand. Finding no one worthy of his daughter, Janaka had vowed that only the man who could string Shiva's bow could marry her. Now Vishvamitra had introduced Rama to the king and he warmed to this powerful and god-like prince, and decided to invite him to attempt the feat.

'If you can string the bow, I promise you the hand of my daughter Sita,' he said.

Janaka ordered the bow to be brought out of the city and placed at the centre of the sacrificial ground. This was no simple task, for it required hundreds of men to move it. It was kept in an iron chest mounted on eight wheels. Slowly the chest was dragged out towards the centre of the ground. As news spread of the king's invitation to Rama, a great crowd assembled. The chest was finally brought before them and opened to reveal the great bow. On a sign from Vishvamitra, Rama stepped forward and grasped it firmly, saying:

'This venerable bow which belonged to Lord Shiva is now in my hand. I will lift it and see how heavy it is, and try and string it.'

Without effort Rama lifted the bow and tossed it on his palm. Before the astonished gaze of the crowd he deftly strung it and began to bend it. He bent it back into a great arc until suddenly, with an explosive report, it snapped, sending out shock waves so powerful they knocked down many of the onlookers.

'Sita is won,' declared Janaka. 'Rama has shown himself to be a man of inconceivable strength. My daughter is dearer to me than life itself, but I now give her to Rama. He will bring fame and fortune to the house of Videha.'

Watched by his guru Vishvamitra, Rama draws the great bow of Shiva and is garlanded by the princess Sita.

Janaka was so excited he wanted to perform the marriage ceremony immediately, but first he sent swift messengers to the court of Emperor Dasaratha to tell him the good news and invite him to come quickly.

Ayodhya lay three days' ride away. Soon Dasaratha heard all that had passed at Janaka's court. Not only were his sons safe after successfully defeating the demons of the night, but they had reached Ayodhya where Rama had achieved the impossible – he had won Sita's hand!

Dasaratha wasted no time. The very next day a caravan of gifts set off under armed guard, closely followed by the emperor's personal party in chariots and palanquins protected by his army. When they reached Mithila they set up camp beside the festival ground, where Janaka made them welcome. Rama and Lakshmana hurried to touch Dasaratha's feet, and the proud father, after offering thanks and prayers for the future happiness of his son and daughter-in-law, slept that night in peace.

Janaka had a second daughter named Urmila, and his younger brother, Kusadhvaja, had two daughters named Mandavi and Srutakirti. All were of marriageable age. It was soon decided to form a grand alliance between the two royal dynasties by uniting the four sons of the house of Iksvaku with the four daughters of the house of Videha.

'Through marriage we will be joined with ties of love,' pronounced Janaka. In celebration, Dasaratha gave costly gifts and thousands of cows with gold-plated horns to the brahmanas of Mithila. Then sacred fires were lit in a pavilion decorated with flowers, golden dishes, jars of water and earthen bowls full of grains. Priests offered incense and ceremonial articles of worship while intoning sacred hymns from the Vedas.

Sita, dazzlingly beautiful and decorated with priceless jewels, was escorted by her father into the pavilion to take her seat next to Rama.

'Here is Sita, my daughter and the daughter of the earth, who will help you discharge your sacred duties. Take her hand in yours, Rama. She will ever be devoted to you and you alone and will follow you like a shadow,' announced Janaka. Rama took Sita's hand. Celestial drums echoed in the sky, and flower petals rained down from the heavens.

One by one the other couples were united: Urmila with Lakshmana, Mandavi with Bharata and Srutakirti with Satrughna. The four brothers led their brides clockwise around the sacred fire three times to the accompaniment of singing and the sound of musical instruments. When all was done, the newly-married couples retired to the privacy of their tents, while the assembled hosts of Mithila and Ayodhya celebrated late into the night.

Rama and his father soon left Mithila in a great procession, laden with gifts of dowry. Vishvamitra departed for the Himalayas, his task complete. The great procession wound its way homeward to Ayodhya, where joyous celebrations were held to welcome the returning emperor and his sons with their brides. Flags and festoons fluttered from tall buildings that looked like the snow-capped peaks of the Himalayas.

Crowds came out to meet them and threw flower petals on the ground. Dasaratha's queens lovingly embraced the princesses and took them by the hand to their private apartments. The princesses, showing proper respect for their elders and being devoted to their husbands, lived happily in their new homes.

For Rama and Lakshmana life was kind. In the company of their illustrious guru Vishvamitra, they had made the passage from youth to manhood, had learned the arts of mystic weapons and had gained beautiful wives. They now lived peacefully as dutiful sons and husbands amidst their friends and relatives.

Two royal dynasties unite as the princes of the House of Ikshaku marry the princesses of the house of Videha: Rama to Sita, Lakshmana to Urmila, Bharata to Mandavi and Satrughna to Srutakirti.

THE SECOND BOOK

Ayodhya Kanda

On the eve of his coronation as the ruler of Ayodhya, Rama becomes
the victim of a plot to banish him. The picture shows Sita and
Rama, with his brother Lakshmana, being driven to the forest where
Rama must live for fourteen years. The citizens of Ayodhya,
abandoned by their future king, follow the party into exile. The
chariot is driven by Rama's faithful attendant Sumantra and
flies the emblem of the Iksvaku royal dynasty. In preparation for
life in the forest, Rama and Lakshmana have put aside their royal
robes and donned the simple dress of ascetics.

BANISHMENT
A KING IN WAITING

AMA ONLY EVER SPOKE the truth. He was grateful for the smallest favour received from others but never took offence from their actions. He understood people and knew how to encourage and correct them, so that they felt appreciated when they were with him. He always kept a positive outlook on life and had a natural sense of the right time and place for everything.

Although he was already far advanced in knowledge he continued to study science, politics and economics, as well as military arts. He wanted to protect his people from all harm, so he learned battle strategies and military command, and in personal combat none could defeat him. Besides all this he still found time to enjoy himself and was a keen patron of music and the arts and an accomplished rider. For all these reasons he shone before all like the Sun god, and all his people loved him.

Not surprisingly, of all his sons Dasaratha loved Rama the most. Emperor Dasaratha was getting old, and seeing how well Rama was doing he decided to pass control of the kingdom over to him. Bad omens had been seen recently, which further convinced him that he should place responsibility for the kingdom into younger and more capable hands. He called together his ministers and advisers and put it to them that it was time to hand over to Rama, but he did not invite Bharata to be present. One reason for this was that Bharata was far away, staying with his uncle Yudhajit, in the state of Kekaya. But there was another reason. Dasaratha had once promised to Kaikeyi's father that her son would be crowned king of Ayodhya. In view of this, he thought it best not to give Bharata the opportunity to object to Rama's coronation.

'After thousands of years in the service of my people my body is worn out and my mind exhausted,' Dasaratha's voice rumbled like distant thunder. 'I now wish to install Rama as king.' He paused. 'Does anyone wish to speak?'

The assembly shifted uneasily. They had to choose their words carefully. How could they show their enthusiasm for Rama without appearing to suggest that the emperor was indeed growing old?

'Mother Earth wants Rama as her guardian,' spoke up Vasistha, 'therefore she has inspired you to think in this way. If it is her wish and yours, then it is also ours. Let Rama be our protector.' Dasaratha seemed pleased with his answer.

'Then let us make haste. Now is a good time for the ceremony. The trees are in blossom and spring is upon us.'

So it was decided. Priests were sent for and hasty preparations began. Ingredients were gathered: white flowers from the meadows, dried paddy, grains, curds, ghee, honey, fragrant oils, gold and precious stones.

'Call the royal guard, decorate the gateways, let the dancers perform. Tomorrow the moon stands in conjunction with the auspicious star Pusya and there is no time to lose,' decreed Dasaratha. When all was underway he called aside his personal assistant, Sumantra, and spoke quietly to him, 'Bring Rama to see me.'

Rama prostrated himself full-length before his father and waited for the familiar touch of his hand. Dasaratha drew his son to him and hugged him long before sitting him on an ornate seat. He loved to look at Rama.

'I am getting old. I have done all I had to do for the gods, the sages, the brahmanas, the people and for myself. But still there is one thing that remains: I must install you as my successor. I have decided that you should be crowned king. The date for your coronation is fixed for tomorrow.'

Rama listened quietly, taking in his father's words. He enjoyed life as a royal prince and had no wish for this sudden change. But his father's word was law and his deep sense of duty and his love for the old man who had always shown him such affection bound him absolutely. To question his wishes would be unthinkable.

'Always be humble, control your senses and avoid anger. Lay up stocks of wealth and food grains. Keep your courtiers happy.' Dasaratha went on with his good advice while Rama listened respectfully. When the interview was finished, he hurried home to tell Sita the news.

Meanwhile, news spread through the city. As Rama returned to his house crowds pressed around to congratulate him. He arrived home and was searching for Sita to tell her about the coronation when he was surprised to see Sumantra again and to hear that the emperor had called for him a second time. Concerned, he hastened to his father.

'My dreams are troubled by omens, meteors have been sighted, and my astrologers have warned that the planets are against me,' Dasaratha told him. 'They say I must take advantage of tomorrow's favourable moon to crown you before it is too late. I am worried about Bharata. He is your loyal and honest brother and he is far away, but he may lay claim to the throne. We must be on our guard tonight. To ward off bad fortune you and Sita should observe a fast through the night and sleep on the bare floor.'

Quickly now Rama went in search of Sita. He found her attending his mother in the temple. Kausalya had long wanted her son crowned, and now her prayers had been answered. Silently she sat in grateful meditation on Vishnu, the Lord of the Heart. Becoming aware of her son's presence, she joyfully embraced him.

'O Rama, may you live long, and may your enemies be destroyed! Now all my sacrifices and prayers to Lord Vishnu have been fulfiled.'

Lakshmana came in and bowed. Rama put his arm around him and said, 'Rule with me. This blessing is for both of us.' Then taking leave, he and Sita made their way home.

THE AVATARS OF VISHNU

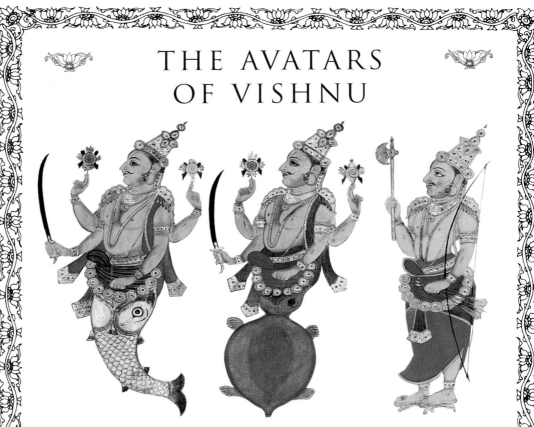

Three avatars of Vishnu (from left to right): Matsya, Kurma and Parasurama.

THE TEN incarnations, or avatars, of Vishnu are a recurrent theme in Vedic literature. Vishnu enters this world to restore its balance, described below by Krishna, the original Vishnu:

Whenever there is a decline in religion, and a rise of irreligion, I incarnate myself. To protect the good, to destroy the wicked, and to re-establish religious principles, I appear in every age.

BHAGAVAD GITA 4.7–8

The ten avatars of Vishnu are: Matsya the fish, who saved all creatures from the universal flood; Kurma the tortoise, who helped the gods gain immortality; Varaha the boar, who rescued the earth from the bottom of the universe; Narasimha the man-lion, who killed the demon Hiranya Kasipu; Vamana the dwarf, who defeated the demon Bali; Parasurama, who defeated the war-like kings; Rama, who killed the demon Ravana; Balarama, brother of Krishna; Buddha, who taught compassion; and Kalki, who will come at the end of time to vanquish evil and inaugurate a new cycle of the universe.

At Rama's palace there were scenes of celebration. Soon Vasistha arrived, sweeping up to the inner gate in his chariot and hurrying inside. Dasaratha had sent him with further counsel.

'There is no going back on this now, Rama. It is most important that you observe the fast according to the proper rules given in the sacred texts.'

After Vasistha left, Sita and Rama lit a sacred fire and made offerings to Vishnu. Then they spread grass mats on the bare floor of the temple and lay down to sleep, thinking only of Lord Vishnu.

TREACHERY

Manthara stood on the roof of the royal palace surveying the scene below. She had heard nothing about Rama's coronation, but she could tell from the flags, the freshly-watered streets, the commotion and noise that something was happening.

'Have you heard? Tomorrow the emperor is to install Rama on the throne.' The words, spoken joyfully by Rama's old nurse, who had just appeared on the roof, hit Manthara's ears like a thunderclap. To her alone in Ayodhya this news was not wonderful. She was Queen Kaikeyi's aged personal maidservant. When Kaikeyi had married Dasaratha, Manthara had come with her as part of the royal household and she was fiercely loyal to her mistress, particularly as her deformity gave her few other friends: she was a hunchback.

She hurried down to find her mistress as usual reclining in her bedroom.

'Get up!' she scolded. 'This is no time to sleep. Your luck is about to evaporate like a river in the dry season. In the absence of your son Bharata your deceitful husband plans to install Rama on the throne. You must act quickly to protect your rights!'

Kaikeyi was bemused at this statement. She looked upon Rama as her own son. His good fortune was hers, and would be shared with all his brothers.

'You are the bearer of joy, Manthara. Why should I be unhappy to hear this?'

'Foolish woman, what is there to celebrate? Don't you see? Once Rama is king your son will be powerless and you will be forced to serve Queen Kausalya.' Manthara knew that Kaikeyi, as the youngest of Dasaratha's wives, was not fond of Kausalya. But these words made Kaikeyi indignant.

'Rama is full of virtue and deserves to be king. Besides he is the eldest brother and it is his right. He will look after Bharata and me as he would his own mother. Already he serves me more than he does her. Anyway, Bharata can still be king. After a hundred years when Rama retires, he will hand over to Bharata, as Dasaratha has to him.'

'How can you be so stupid as to think Bharata will ever get the throne? Once Rama is king the succession will go to his son, as it always does, and Bharata will be excluded forever from the royal line. Rama will more likely send Bharata into exile. Rama should be sent away instead, and Bharata should have the throne. You must act to protect Bharata and yourself from the schemes of your co-wife. Find a way to give Bharata the throne and banish Rama.'

Kaikeyi heard this with increasing alarm. It was true that she had always wanted Bharata to be king, especially because Dasaratha had promised it so, and she did resent Kausalya's seniority. Now Manthara's crooked words fed her fears and ignited a resentment born of long frustration. Her lethargy turned to anger.

'Perhaps you speak the truth, Manthara. Maybe Rama should be sent away and Bharata put on the throne. But how on earth could it be done?'

'You yourself have the means, you told me in the past. Must I remind you?' Kaikeyi got up from her bed. Her interest was definitely aroused.

'Once when Dasaratha was severely wounded on the battlefield, you saved his life by taking him away to a safe place. At that time he offered you two boons. You said you would ask for them later, to which he said, "So be it!" You told me this long ago and I have treasured it ever since, waiting for the right time to help you. Now you should ask for these two boons to be granted. First, ask that Bharata be put on the throne. Second, demand that Rama be banished from the kingdom for fourteen years,' exclaimed Manthara.

Kaikeyi listened with excitement as Manthara told her to enter her chamber of wrath, her private room for anger and depression, throw off her ornaments and finery, loosen her hair and lie on the floor. When her husband would find her there she must weep and wail and wait for him to offer her what she wanted.

'He will offer you jewels and gifts. Do not accept them. Fix your mind only on the throne for Bharata and banishment for Rama.'

Manthara made her put on old clothes and sent her to the chamber of wrath. The delicate queen untied her hair and threw herself upon the ground, scattering her ornaments about her. Tossing from side to side she began to work herself into a frenzy.

'If Rama becomes king your life will be misery and your son will surely be killed!' Manthara goaded her.

'Either Bharata will be crowned or I will eat nothing and stay here until I die,' said Kaikeyi. Her face darkened by rage and her heart poisoned by Manthara's arrows of hatred, she awaited her husband.

Dasaratha had just seen Rama for the second time and evening was approaching. He had been issuing orders all day and at last he felt confident that all was in hand for the coronation. Now he looked forward to the enjoyable task of telling his dear Kaikeyi the exciting news. As was his habit he went to find her in her bedroom.

Kaikeyi's bedchamber was empty, her bed unused. He found one of her maids who told him nervously that she was in her chamber of wrath. In dismay he entered the darkened room and found her sprawled on the floor, like a creeper torn from a tree, weeping piteously. He knelt beside her, but she pushed him away.

'My beloved, who has upset you? What is wrong? Let me put it right. If someone needs to be punished I will punish them, or if someone must be rewarded I will reward them.' The queen took no notice and continued to weep. 'I promise on my honour that

I will do whatever pleases you. I rule an empire stretching from the southern Deccan to the Himalayas, from east of Bengal to west of Rajasthan. Whatever you want is yours.' She turned to him. 'No one has insulted me,' she sobbed, 'but there is something I must have. Promise you will give it. Give me your word and I shall tell you what it is.' She had Dasaratha at her mercy.

'My dear, I promise you shall have what you want. I swear on my beloved Rama, without whom I could not live for even a day. I swear I will satisfy your desire. Please let me make you happy again.' Helplessly the emperor was drawn into Kaikeyi's trap.

'Indra and the gods have heard your oath. The moon and sun bear witness to your words. Now listen to me.' Kaikeyi's voice hardened. 'Remember when I saved your life and you offered me two boons? Now I want them. If you refuse me I promise I will die. My first request is for Bharata to be installed on the throne in place of Rama. My second is for Rama to be sent this very day to Dandaka Forest for fourteen years to live as a hermit.'

Dasaratha could not believe his ears. All day he had felt a sense of foreboding which now turned to a throbbing in his head and pain in his heart. He collapsed on the bare floor beside his queen and began to murmur.

'O pity! Pity! Your words are cruel. What harm has Rama ever done you? When

In her chamber of wrath, Queen Kaikeyi rolls on the floor in hysteria,
then demands two boons from the emperor.

the whole world loves him why should I send him away? Life might go on without the sun or water, but I cannot live without Rama. I can't believe you mean what you say. This is not you speaking, but some evil spirit that has entered you. I might agree to put Bharata on the throne, but I will never banish Rama. Take pity on me. I am old and weak. You can have anything I possess, but without Rama I will die.' But the emperor's weakness only served to strengthen Kaikeyi's resolve.

'You have given me your oath. Are you going back on your promise?' she tormented him. 'Your word has no value? Banish Rama or I shall drink poison.'

In vain Dasaratha tried to reason with this cruel queen, by turns groaning and pleading. How would Rama, who knew only fine food and soft beds, survive alone in the forest? Rama was so noble and obedient that if asked he would go at once without complaint, but what of Sita and Kausalya? Surely they would die of broken hearts without him. Indeed who would wish to stay in Ayodhya if he were gone? Even Bharata would not stay. And Dasaratha would be ridiculed and die. Kaikeyi would be left alone to preside over the collapse of the empire. But the woman's heart was hard and cold and his words useless. Spent, he collapsed at her feet, a broken man.

Darkness fell and the palace became silent. Dasaratha lay unconscious. As the long night passed, he drifted in and out of wakefulness, pleading and whimpering, and dreading the arrival of dawn. The queen, however, was alert with angry determination. As the sky lightened she commanded Dasaratha to send for Rama.

Unaware of these terrible events, Vasistha, who was the emperor's family priest, boarded his chariot in the bright morning and made his way to see Dasaratha, followed by priests carrying ingredients for the ceremony. Reaching the palace he sent Sumantra to announce his arrival. Sumantra was surprised to discover that the emperor was not yet up, having passed the night in Kaikeyi's quarters. Passing the queen's personal attendants, who dared not stop him, Sumantra entered the inner chambers.

'O king, awake, for today is a glorious day,' he called. 'As the sun wakes the world so do I wake you. Vasistha is here and all is ready. Come and order the installation of Rama.' From the shadows emerged the emperor, red-eyed and feeble.

'I am not asleep, Sumantra. Silence, please. You are only making things worse.' The emperor collapsed onto a couch and Kaikeyi stepped forward.

'He was unable to sleep last night in anticipation of today's coronation,' said Kaikeyi. 'Now he is exhausted. Call Rama to come here at once.' Sumantra hesitated, waiting for the emperor's approval.

'Do as she says – bring Rama,' murmured the emperor. Sumantra hurried to fetch him.

Hearing that his father wanted him, Rama came out of his palace like a lion from his mountain cave. Joined by Lakshmana he mounted his chariot, inlaid with gems and gold, and moved in state procession through the city. The crowd followed him right up to the inner gate of the palace, where they waited for his return as the ocean waits for the moon.

Rama went inside with Lakshmana. As soon as he saw his father he knew something was terribly wrong. He was sitting with Kaikeyi on her bed, his face black with despair like the sun in an eclipse. Rama bowed at his feet. Dasaratha could not speak save to falteringly repeat the name 'Rama', and his eyes were blinded with tears. Rama turned to Kaikeyi in alarm.

'What has upset my father? Rama demanded. 'Have I angered him in some way? Why is he in such a state?'

'The emperor is not angry. He has something to ask of you but he cannot bring himself to say the words. If you promise to carry out his wish I will reveal it to you. On his own he will never tell you.'

'Mother, you know that I will do anything for my father. If he wishes I will drink poison. Tell me his wish and I shall execute it. Rama never goes back on his word!'

'Long ago your father offered me two boons, and now I am claiming them. I have asked him to install Bharata on the throne in your place and to exile you to Dandaka Forest for fourteen years where you are to live as an ascetic. Now you know why your father cannot look you in the face.'

These words made Lakshmana recoil in anger and dismay, but Rama heard them without flinching. His voice remained even-tempered as he replied:

'If the emperor has promised you this then without hesitation I shall go to the forest.'

Kaikeyi was delighted to find Rama so cooperative. Shamelessly she pushed home her advantage, urging him not to waste time in getting ready to leave.

'I am not attached to worldly comfort, and I will happily live in the forest for fourteen years. I do not need to hear it personally from my father. Your word as my mother

SADHUS & ASHRAMS

During his exile Rama met many sadhus, holy men or women, living in the forest. In modern India, Sadhus are still an important part of Hindu life. They practice detachment from the world, following the advice of Krishna in the Bhagavad Gita:

'Happiness and distress appear and disappear like the passing of winter and summer. They arise from the perception of the senses and you must learn to tolerate them without being disturbed.'

BHAGAVAD GITA 2.14

This renunciation sets an example to the rest of society and makes sadhus the object of veneration to ordinary people. Even today a genuine sadhu ranks higher than anyone in Hindu society.

An advanced sadhu may become a guru and accept disciples who live with their teacher in the ashram, or place of spiritual shelter. They follow a daily routine beginning before dawn with bathing, worship and study of the scriptures. Sadhus and their disciples often take vows of celibacy.

is sufficient, and I will leave today. Make sure Bharata is brought here at once to protect the kingdom and look after my poor ageing father.' So saying Rama bowed before his weeping father and the hateful Kaikeyi and strode purposefully out of the palace, taking with him Lakshmana, whose eyes were brimming with tears of anger.

Rama emerged into the sunlight before the waiting crowd. He sent away his chariot and royal attendants and insisted on walking on foot to see his mother. As he entered her chamber, he saw that she was in the midst of her morning worship, praying for blessings for his installation. Happily, she embraced him. Rama held her tight.

'Mother, I have painful news for you. The emperor has decided to give the throne to Bharata and has sent me away to the forest for fourteen years where I must live as a hermit, feeding on roots and herbs.'

The queen trembled. The blood drained from her face. She opened her mouth but no sound came out. Rama caught her as she fell and held her in his arms.

'My son!' she stammered, 'I would rather have stayed childless than have to hear such words. I cannot bear the pain of losing you. Let death take me.'

Lakshmana could stay silent no longer.

'The emperor is out of his mind. He is so attached to Kaikeyi that he does not know what he is saying,' he burst out. 'No son should have to obey a senile old man when he is in this state. I should kill him rather than see Rama go.'

'Listen to your brother, Rama! Such terrible words have never been spoken in this family. And if you leave I will fast to death. Give up this madness,' said his mother.

'Mother, this is not madness. This is my sacred duty. I must obey my father. Don't despair – I shall return after fourteen years.' Rama was calm and unmoved. He turned to his brother. 'Truth is the source of our strength, Lakshmana, and must never be given up. There is no use in making threats.' Kausalya cried without control; Lakshmana shook with anger; and Rama stood between them.

'Lakshmana, you must understand that truthfulness and honour come before every-thing. I am bound by my father's order. I would rather live in the forest with nothing than rule a kingdom at the cost of my honour. Do not blame Kaikeyi or the emperor for this turn of events. How could Kaikeyi have ever thought of such a thing herself? It is not her doing. They are both

Dasaratha begs Queen Kaikeyi to ask for anything but Rama's banishment (see page 40).

under the control of providence. I am also under the same control. I accept this as the will of God.'

Lakshmana, however, was wild-eyed and ready to defend Rama by force. 'This is a conspiracy, don't you see? he cried out. 'This story of vows has been fabricated to get rid of you. If it is true, why did we not hear it before? As for your honour, your surrender to fate will be interpreted as weakness and your piety ridiculed. We must fight for what we know is right, not meekly surrender. Tell me who your enemies are and I will destroy them. They will never send you away.' Lakshmana's voice broke with emotion as he wiped away tears of frustration. Rama caught his hand and tried to soothe him.

'I know you love me, Lakshmana, and I know you want to help me. Instead of threatening violence on my behalf, use your energies to get everything ready for my departure. I must leave as soon as possible.'

Kausalya saw it was useless to try to dissuade Rama. She felt the misery building up inside her, threatening to consume her like a forest fire. She pleaded with Rama that if he must go, let him take her with him. She would look after him and prepare his food. But Rama was adamant.

'Poor father will not survive if both of us desert him. Dear mother, you know that a woman's duty is to serve her husband.'

'Go then, and may the gods protect you. I will wait for your return, my beloved son!'

She gathered flowers and incense and chanted hymns, imploring Vishnu to protect her boy. She tied on his wrist an amulet blessed with sacred mantras. Her eyes streaming tears, she held him in her embrace, and smiled bravely. 'I can see you now, dear boy, returning from the forest – your face shining as you run towards me, your arms reaching out to embrace me. You are dressed in forest barks with leaves in your hair.'

Rama loosened her hold and made to go.

'Hurry back my child,' she cried, 'I cannot wait for long.'

He slipped from her grasp.

LEAVING AYODHYA

Sita waited for her husband to return from seeing his father, full of expectation for the coronation ceremony ahead. When Rama at last appeared it was obvious that he was not his usual self. Whereas Rama had stayed calm with his father and mother, when he came to see Sita he could no longer restrain his feelings. He had intended to leave her behind, but found it hard to keep his resolve.

'What is wrong, my Lord? You have come without your royal attendants who should be with you on this special day, and you are pale and trembling.'

'My beloved Sita, father has seen fit to send me into exile and to give the throne to Bharata.' Rama told her all that had happened as she sat in stunned silence.

'While I am gone you will be under the care of Bharata. Be sure not to praise me in my absence, as this may provoke him. Honour my father and mother as well as Kaikeyi and Sumitra, who have always been my well-wishers. Look upon Bharata and Satrughna as your own brothers.'

'Stop this!' interrupted Sita. 'I am not staying here without you, so there is no use in your telling me what to do here. A wife's place is by her husband, and you are my only protector. Do not insult me by suggesting that I will accept the protection of Bharata or anyone else. If you must go to the forest then I will come with you. I will walk ahead, crushing the thorns on the path. Even though the forest is full of dangerous animals I will be happy there with you. I will live on roots and fruits and cause you no trouble. I look forward to seeing the mountains and waterfalls and lakes full of swans and lotus flowers. I long to live in the forest with you.'

Rama tried to dissuade Sita. She had no idea how perilous the forest was.

'I will tell you what the forest is really like. Sharp stones, thorny heaths; the roar of lions and attack of wild beasts; rushing streams, alligators guarding the rivers and ponds; hunger gnaws and mosquitoes bite. In wind and rain you search for food. In darkness scorpions sting and serpents creep among the stones. That is forest life.'

Sita began to cry, but she was still determined, saying: 'When I was a little girl a holy woman once came to our house and I overheard her tell my mother that one day I would live in the forest. It is my destiny. I will not feel the pain when I lie on the forest floor beside you. Leaves or roots will taste like nectar when they come from your hand.' Tears fell like crystals from her lotus eyes. 'We are bound together forever. In the scriptures it is said that a woman stays bound to her husband even in the next life. Either I live with you in the forest or I will die here without you.'

Unable to deny her any longer, Rama took her in his arms. 'Alright. Since this is your destiny, come with me. Together we will vow to give up all comforts and live in the forest on the order of my father. To serve one's father, mother or guru brings the highest reward, even entrance to Goloka, the eternal forest of Krishna. Now be quick and get everything ready. Give gifts to the brahmanas and distribute whatever of ours that is left to our household servants.'

Lakshmana stood by anxiously. Since childhood he and Rama had never been separated. Fighting back his tears he now spoke up.

'If you go to the forest with Sita, then you must take me too. I can go ahead with my bow so that you can wander safely, enjoying the natural beauty. If I stay here without you my life will be empty and useless.'

So it was decided that the three of them would go together into exile.

The three companions went back to the royal palace to take their leave of Dasaratha. News of Rama's banishment had spread among the ordinary people of Ayodhya. It was hard for them to understand what was happening. Why had Dasaratha done this? As the three passed along the street, without Rama's usual company of royal guards and chariots, onlookers felt dismayed. They looked upon Rama as the root of their existence and could not conceive of life without him.

'We will follow Rama,' they said to one another, 'we will turn the forest into Ayodhya and let Ayodhya revert to forest. Kaikeyi will inherit a deserted city, inhabited by wild animals and mice.'

Rama came once more before his father. Dasaratha had called all his wives to be present. Headed by Kausalya they filled the room, many weeping uncontrollably. In their midst the emperor sat on a couch, propped up by pillows, red-eyed and exhausted, showing all the symptoms of a complete breakdown. When he saw Rama he struggled bravely to his feet, but even as Rama approached he began to totter, so that Rama had to catch him and lay him tenderly on the couch. Gently, Rama explained that he, Sita and Lakshmana were ready to leave and that they had come to say goodbye. In desperation, with a low voice trembling with emotion, Dasaratha spoke.

'My senses are quite gone, my son, taken from me by Kaikeyi, and I am powerless. You take charge. Hold me captive and take the throne by force.'

'Be calm, father, you know that I could never do such a thing. I am quite resigned to going away. Please accept all these events as inevitable destiny, and allow Bharata to peacefully rule the kingdom while I am gone.'

'If you are determined to honour my vow, Rama, as I knew you would be, please let your mother and I cherish one last night with you.' But Rama would not stay. He did not want to prolong the pain of parting any longer.

Dasaratha tried to struggle to his feet to give his son a last embrace, but as he did so his fragile frame could take no more. The old man collapsed unconscious on the couch. A great wail went up from all his wives. Even the men present openly wept. Kaikeyi alone seemed unmoved.

'Queen Kaikeyi, you are an evil woman,' cried Sumantra, whose usual cool exterior was shattered by uncontrollable waves of anger. 'You are the murderer of Dasaratha and our whole race. You violate all codes of honour of the Iksvaku house.' He spoke for them all. 'If Rama leaves, we will all leave with him, and you will be left with nothing. All you will achieve in sending him away is to send yourself to hell!'

Kaikeyi's face betrayed no emotion, as if carved from stone. Dasaratha stirred. A new thought occurred to him. In a weak voice he ordered Sumantra to deploy his entire army to accompany Rama to the forest, with provisions of food and gold. With them should go priests, merchants, hunters and the whole entourage of civilization.

Kaikeyi protested bitterly that Ayodhya would be stripped of its wealth and armies, leaving nothing for Bharata. These shameless words provoked even Dasaratha to retaliate that he too would go the forest with Rama, and leave her forever. Rama intervened. 'I have no use for an army or great wealth in the forest. I relinquish all claims to the throne of Ayodhya or any of its possessions. Mother Kaikeyi, please bring us forest clothes, woven from grass and tree-bark, and a spade and basket for gathering roots and herbs. We shall take nothing more, and we shall go alone.'

Without delay Kaikeyi brought what he requested and Lakshmana and Rama changed into the simple robes. Sita, however, was dismayed at such plain garments and had no idea what to do with them. Rama helped her to drape them over her finery. It was a pitiful sight.

Kausalya embraced Sita with bitter tears. Rama consoled his mother. 'Don't despair, dear mother, our exile will soon be over. Fourteen years will slip by even while you are asleep.' Then turning to all his family members and friends gathered around, he went on, 'Please forgive any offences I may have committed. Now I must take leave of you all. Farewell!'

Rama led his two companions as they went first to the emperor, then to Queen Kausalya, bowing and walking around them in respect. Lakshmana tearfully embraced his mother Sumitra, who urged him to serve Sita and Rama as if they were his own mother and father.

Outside a chariot stood waiting for them carrying Sita's ornaments and silk robes, mighty bows and other weapons, a basket and a spade. They boarded it and Sumantra took the reins.

Picking up speed, the chariot headed for the city gates. On the way the people of Ayodhya lined the streets. Moans and cries went up on all sides, and young and old pushed forward to catch hold of the chariot as it passed. Many ran after it, tears streaming down their faces, imploring the driver to slow down so that they could get a good look at the faces of their beloved Rama and Sita.

Dasaratha did his best to follow them. 'Slow down,' he ordered Sumantra.

'Speed up,' commanded Rama. The dust of the chariot's wheels mixed with the people's tears.

Turning, Rama saw Dasaratha slip and fall, unable to get up. Kausalya and his aides bent to help him as he called pitifully for Rama. Rama turned away and did not look back. 'Drive on!' he ordered Sumantra, as they passed through the city gates.

Helped by Kausalya, the emperor got to his feet and reached the edge of the city. He watched the chariot diminish into the distance, followed by a cloud of dust, until all that could be seen was a blur on the horizon. He stayed rooted to the spot, unable to turn away. In front of him on the road he saw the wheel-marks of Rama's chariot, but even as he looked the breeze blew them away, leaving no trace of his passing. Kaikeyi came to take his arm, but he pushed her away.

'No longer are you any relation of mine. I disown you and all your household.'

After a long time he turned to go back. The emperor made his way to the palace with Kausalya. He had eyes for no one and thought only of Rama and hid himself in Kausalya's apartments. A dark cloud settled over Ayodhya. No fires burned and people did not eat. Men's faces were wet with tears and mothers ignored their children. The wind gusted along empty streets while the sun hid behind unseasonal clouds.

In the moonless night, Kausalya sat beside her husband's bed. His breath came fitfully in intermittent gasps. Inside her she felt the fire burn ever hotter, consuming her will to live. Dasaratha reached out in the darkness.

'Kausalya, I can't see you. I have gone blind. Touch me with your hand.'

She took his hand in hers and let out a long piteous wail.

INTO THE FOREST

The chariot kept up speed for a while, with the citizens from Ayodhya desperately straggling behind. White-haired men, bent with age, who thought they could convince Rama to change his mind, were among them. Feeling pity for them, Rama stopped the chariot and continued on foot as far as the river Tamasa, where he halted for the night.

As birds sang evening lullabies the travellers settled on a bed of leaves for their first night out in the open. Rama made sure the horses were well fed, but for himself drank only a little water. He had no appetite for more. Lakshmana could not sleep and sat up all night talking about Rama with Sumantra. Several hours before dawn Rama awoke and was distressed to see the good people of Ayodhya strewn on the bare ground fast asleep. Without disturbing them, Rama and his companions quietly rode their chariot across the swiftly-flowing river, being careful not to leave any tell-tale tracks on the other side. When the poor citizens awoke they searched everywhere for Rama. Unable to find any trace of him they returned to their homes in despair.

Rama pushed on southwards through the cool pre-dawn air, his mind fixed on his father's order. By the time the sun rose he and his companions had left the river far behind. All that day they passed through the fertile lands of Kosala, full of gardens and temples, crossing the rivers Gomati and Syandaki. News went before them and along the way village folk left their fields to implore Rama not to leave. He was unable to check his tears, but sent them back to their work. At last they reached the holy Ganges, whose deep waters, decorated with white lotus flowers and swans, marked

When it is time to say goodbye to his son Rama, Emperor Dasaratha faints with grief and is revived by his queens.

the border of Iksvaku territory. Rama looked back the way they had come to salute the far-off city of Ayodhya, saying: 'When I have honoured my father's vow I will return.'

The chief of those parts was Guha, loyal to the Iksvaku kings. He welcomed Rama and his companions with well-cooked food and soft beds. Yet Rama was still not hungry.

'I have vowed to sleep on the ground and eat only forest fruits and roots,' he told Guha. But he asked him to care for his horses. Lakshmana stayed awake a second night and shared his sorrows with Guha: 'I fear that without Rama the emperor and queen may not have the strength to survive this night.'

Comforted by Guha, he shed hot tears while Rama and Sita slept.

In the morning the two princes treated their hair with sap from the banyan tree and twisted it into top-knots, in the style of forest sages. They put on quivers and loaded their gear into a boat. For Sumantra, the moment of parting had arrived, and he grew visibly distressed when Rama told him he must now go back to Ayodhya.

'The emperor and my mother need you now more than ever. Tell them we are safe and at peace. Embrace Bharata for me and make sure he is properly installed on the throne. Console the people of Ayodhya, for when they see my empty chariot they will know for certain that I have gone to the forest. God speed!'

Lakshmana steadied the boat in the swift-flowing current as Sita nervously stepped in, then they were off, drifting quickly downstream. At the centre of the river Sita spoke softly to the goddess in the waters imploring her to protect Rama during their coming ordeal. Soon they were walking in single file, following the southern bank of the Ganges, with Lakshmana in the lead and Sita protected in the middle.

'Now begins forest life,' said Rama to Sita. 'Today you will walk where no humans live.' That night, as they prepared to sleep beneath the shelter of a great banyan tree, Rama's heart was heavy with thoughts of his mother, and the persecution she would have to endure from Kaikeyi. He cried quietly. Lakshmana came and comforted him and prepared a bed for him and Sita.

'It is best not to grieve, Rama,' he said.

Rama felt strengthened by his brother's words, and neither he nor Lakshmana ever grieved again in the midst of that unending forest.

All the next day they walked steadily within sight of the river. Towards evening they saw ahead of them smoke wafting up through the trees, and heard in the distance rushing waters. They had reached the hermitage of the sage Bharadvaja at the confluence of the Ganges and the Yamuna.

Youthful ascetics greeted them and brought them before their teacher, who sat surrounded by birds and forest animals. He was expecting them, and had made arrangements for them to live there, but Rama declined. Here people would find them out.

'Tell me where we can find a hidden place where Sita will be happy,' he asked.

'There is a sacred mountain called Chitrakoot sixty miles from here whose woods abound with black-tailed monkeys, deer and elephants,' the sage replied. 'Rich supplies of honey, roots and fruits are there, with sheltered caves and waterfalls.'

In the morning Bharadvaja directed them to Chitrakoot, across the Yamuna and two days' walk to the south-west. Rama and Lakshmana built a raft of logs, and on it a seat of cane and rose-apple wood for Sita.

When they reached mid-stream Sita again spoke to the river goddess Yamuna, asking for Rama's safety. Bharadvaja had told them they would reach a great banyan tree, and there they should turn south. When they found it, they stopped for the night.

The next day they continued southwards, along a well-trodden path. Around them were trees laden with scented blossoms, resounding with the buzzing of bees and warbling of birds. As they neared their destination, Lakshmana grew excited.

'Look at the size of the honeycombs and the luscious fruits! Ahead I can see the peaks of Chitrakoot and hear the trumpeting of elephants.'

A sage (Valmiki, for it was he) was waiting for them in his ashram at Chitrakoot with great delight. He gave Sita and Rama a place to sit while Lakshmana busied himself constructing a thatched cottage. When it was complete, Rama built inside it a shrine to the forest guardians and to Vishnu. He consecrated it with Vedic hymns and a sacred fire ceremony. At last, Rama felt released from the pain of the past days and they rested with peaceful hearts.

AYODHYA IN GRIEF

Sumantra watched with a heavy heart as Rama's boat swiftly floated out across the River Ganges. He camped beside the river for two more nights, hoping for Rama's return. But when word came to him that the three travellers had been seen on the path to Chitrakoot, he gave up hope and set off back to Ayodhya. Two days later, with empty chariot and weeping horses, he entered the desolate city.

The emperor and queen pressed him for news of Rama. They wanted every last detail, hoping against hope for Rama's return. Sumantra delivered Rama's messages but he only succeeded in confirming what everyone already feared:

Restrained by his wives, the despairing Dasaratha bids farewell to Rama, his favourite son.

49

Rama, Sita and Lakshmana would not be seen again in Ayodhya for fourteen years.

Faced with the awful finality of what he had done, the emperor was lost in an ocean of despair in which his breathing was a whirlpool, his crying was crashing waves, Kaikeyi's words were alligators and the opposite shore was Sita and Rama.

'Take me to Rama and Sita,' begged Kausalya, 'take me there quickly on your chariot, or I shall instead go to the house of Death. Your foolishness has destroyed us all,' she accused her husband bitterly. Then, in remorse, she took his trembling hands: 'My love, I should not speak to you so. Grief has destroyed my patience. These last five nights have seemed like five years.' But her harsh words penetrated the emperor's dull consciousness like a sharp sword. He fell into an uneasy sleep in which distant memories flooded his mind.

Once more he was a young prince, proud and handsome, and he loved to hunt. One night he ventured alone into the jungle to practice the skill of shooting at an unseen target, aiming by sound only, and waited in the darkness beside a pond. He heard a gurgling sound which he thought was the sound of an elephant drinking, and released a serpent-like arrow. From the darkness he heard a human cry. In horror, he ran forward and discovered a young boy pierced through the heart by his arrow. The sound he had heard was the sound of the boy filling a water-pot, which now lay beside him. Blood trickled from the boy's mouth.

'O shame!' cried the boy, 'who has done this terrible deed? I have no enemy and I am the only support of my parents who are blind and invalid. I came here to draw water for them, but now I am mortally wounded and can no longer protect them.'

The boy begged Prince Dasaratha to remove the arrow which bit into him like fire. The prince pulled out the arrow, but as soon as he did so the boy stared at him with silent agony, and died.

Alone in the darkness and sick with remorse, Dasaratha filled the pot and took it to the boy's parents whom he found nearby. He knew he must tell them the awful truth.

'By accident I have killed your son. Now you must punish me.'

The blind old man spoke.

'Without our son we cannot survive. Tomorrow we will die on his funeral pyre. Because you did this in ignorance you will not be punished in hell, but because you have given us such pain I curse you also to lose your son in old age, and the pain of your loss will kill you.'

Dasaratha woke with a start. It was night and he was alone and cold. In a broken voice he called for Kausalya.

'Touch me! I cannot see you. I am about to die.'

But Kausalya heard nothing.

'My memory is fading. I cannot see my beloved Rama! Fortunate are those who will see his sweet face as he returns from the forest like the autumn moon after the rains. I hear nothing, my hands are numb. I feel myself slipping away. My darling Rama, where are you! O cruel Kaikeyi!' With these words on his lips, the emperor left this world in the dead of night.

Ayodhya had no emperor. A land without an emperor is like a dried-up river. Rains cease to fall; sons disobey fathers; wives disrespect husbands; young girls walk in fear of violation; doors are locked at night; merchants do not flourish, and holy men are neglected. Without its emperor, Ayodhya was a night without stars.

Kausalya found the dead emperor and cried out, 'Kaikeyi, you have your wish: the kingdom is yours. I shall follow my dead husband into the flames.'

Ministers took away the body of Dasaratha and preserved it in oil until a son could be brought to perform the funeral rites. They decided that Bharata should be made king, and they sent messengers to Kekaya to fetch him and his younger brother Satrughna. The messengers rode with lavish gifts for the Kekaya king, through four days and three nights.

In Kekaya, Bharata was uneasy. His mind was filled with disturbing images from his dreams. He saw his father lying in a muddy pool. He saw the earth shake, volcanoes erupt and the moon fall from the sky. Then he saw his father, garlanded with red flowers, dragged southwards in a chariot pulled by donkeys.

When the messengers arrived from Ayodhya he was not surprised. They revealed nothing, only that he was needed urgently. But he knew. When such things are dreamed, one prepares for death.

Burdened with gifts from the Kekaya monarch and accompanied by a small army,

From the right: The royals leave behind their loyal followers; they spend their first night alone in the open; they are ferried across the Ganges by Guha's men; and Lakshmana prepares a meal in the forest. On the extreme right, Sumantra returns to Ayodhya with his chariot empty.

51

he set off in convoy for Ayodhya, reaching there seven days later, ten days after the demise of his father, and fifteen days after Rama's departure. Arriving at the gates, he saw the city streets empty and unswept and his apprehension grew.

Immediately Bharata rushed to his father's apartments, but they were empty. He went to find Kaikeyi.

'Where is father? Is he not with you?'

'O son! Your father is no more.'

Hearing the dreaded words, Bharata fell down and began beating the floor with his powerful arms.

'Get up! You must be strong. You are now the king.'

Kaikeyi told Bharata her good news: Rama exiled, the throne given to Bharata, and Dasaratha dead.

'I have done all this for you, my dear son. Now the kingdom is yours, just as you always wanted.'

Bharata slowly took all this in. 'You have done this to please me?' he asked incredulously. 'What possible wish could I have to take the throne from Rama and see my father dead? Rama is the source of my strength, what can I do without him?' He paced back and forth and then spoke with resolve. 'I will bring Rama back from the forest and go into exile in his place.' Then his anger rose and he roared like a mountain lion.

'O cruel woman, you have shamed our royal house, you have driven away my

KARMA & REBIRTH

VEDIC WISDOM teaches that each living being in this world is an eternal soul inhabiting a temporary body. The individual soul, called atma, is a particle of Vishnu's own spiritual nature. Each soul has its own desires to enjoy the world, and to fulfil these desires it enters the cycle of rebirth, called samsara. When the soul leaves one body that body dies, then the soul is born into another body, like an actor changing clothes. Moving from body to body in search of happiness, the soul passes through all forms of life, from insect to god.

'As the self passes in this body from childhood to youth to old age, so when this body dies the self passes into another body. The wise are not deluded by this change.'

BHAGAVAD GITA 2.13

The law of action and reaction, called karma, governs the movements of all beings, rewarding and punishing their good or bad behaviour. For example, taking life brings bad karma, and feeding the hungry brings good karma.

beloved brother, and you have killed your own husband. You are my enemy disguised as my mother and I no longer wish to speak with you. You should either leave this place or kill yourself.'

A crowd gathered to hear Bharata vent his anger. Kausalya accused him bitterly.

'Now you can take the throne which your mother worked so hard to get for you. I am sure you will be very happy. If you like, you can send me away too. I will go to join Rama.'

Cut to the core to hear these words, Bharata swore his innocence. He spoke not just to her but to all of Ayodhya with words that seared into the hearts of all present.

'I knew nothing of my mother's plans, nor did I ever desire the throne. Whoever wished Rama to be banished is cursed a hundred times,' he repeated over and over again. 'Let them be perpetually barred from heaven; let them forget all the sacred scriptures; let them suffer constant illness; let them go mad and wander as beggars…' Becoming more and more distraught, at last he fell headlong on the floor.

Kausalya, in tears, hurried forward to comfort the stricken youth. Taking his head on her lap, she soothed him with gentle words.

'My child, stop now. You are innocent of any fault. Be comforted.'

The next day Vasistha urged Bharata to perform his duty as the eldest available son of Dasaratha. The funeral must be performed. A pyre was built at the royal cremation ground beside the river Sarayu and Bharata walked in procession with Dasaratha's body, which was decked with jewels and flowers. He lit the fire and watched as his father's remains were reduced to ashes. Then, as was the custom, he stayed with his family in seclusion for twelve days of mourning. On the thirteenth day he returned to the cremation ground to collect his father's whitened bones. Crying inconsolably, he and Satrughna tossed the bones and ashes into the river.

'Life and death, joy and sorrow, gain and loss,' intoned Vasistha. 'These dualities cannot be avoided. Learn to accept what you cannot change and give up sorrow.'

IN SEARCH OF RAMA

Vasistha wanted normal life restored to the troubled kingdom, so he urged Bharata to accept the throne.

'You are now the heir, as ordained by your father. Take what is rightfully yours.'

But Bharata was not to be tempted. 'The throne, and I myself, belong to Rama. I will bring him back to Ayodhya and put him on the throne, while I take his place in the forest.'

Accordingly, Bharata ordered a great expedition to go in search of Rama. It was to be made up of a vast army of elephants, chariots and cavalry. To prepare the way, teams of engineers worked day and night to transform the path to the Ganges into a broad highway lined with trees, with magnificent pavilions along the way. All this activity inspired the people of Ayodhya. With Bharata as their commander, they felt renewed hope, and the leading citizens joined the expedition in festive mood.

Early one morning when all was ready, Bharata, the hero of the Iksvaku race, set off followed by the vast host of Iksvaku: archers borne in chariots; richly decorated elephants; mounted cavalry; and in their midst the three queens of Ayodhya riding in chariots of royal splendour. All minds were fixed on the joyful prospect of finding Rama. Soon they reached the Ganges, where the huge company halted for the night.

Guha, the tribal chief loyal to Rama, saw the army entering his territory and was uneasy, wondering at Bharata's motive in pursuing Rama with an army. Bearing gifts of honey and mango-pulp, he went down to meet him.

'How could I have any evil intentions towards my elder brother, who is just like a father to me?' Bharata assured him. 'We want Rama to come back and be king.' Bharata appeared confident of achieving this, but secretly he wondered whether he could succeed. Reassured of Bharata's good intentions, Guha offered to help them across the Ganges and guide them to their next stop, the hermitage of Bharadvaja.

That night Guha showed Bharata and his mothers the place where Rama and Sita had spent the night, guarded by Lakshmana.

'See here the blades of grass crushed as Rama slept,' said Bharata, 'and here the strands of gold thread from Sita's cloth which have stuck to the hard ground where she lay. A devoted wife will undergo any hardship in the company of her lord. For myself, I vow to sleep on the bare ground and live on fruits and roots in the forest for the remainder of Rama's exile, so that his vow will be fulfiled.'

Bharata could not hide his emotions and fell to the ground in tears. He was consoled by Kausalya, who hugged him close to her breast.

'Be strong, Bharata. You are now my only support.'

The Iksvaku host crossed the River Ganges on five hundred boats supplied by Guha. As far as the eye could see the river teemed with boats and rafts of all sizes, loaded with men, women and horses, while elephants swam like glistening mountains through the throng.

Following the path taken by Rama, they soon reached the hermitage of Bharadvaja. Bharata halted the army and went forward alone to meet the holy sage. Again his motives were questioned.

'I know you to be Rama's brother,' spoke Bharadvaja, 'who must now be ruling in his place. I trust you come in peace.'

'I beg you not to think of me as a threat,' protested Bharata. 'My only motive is to bring Rama back to Ayodhya.'

The sage was pleased to hear this and happily extended his hospitality to Bharata and all his company.

'You are a simple hermit,' said Bharata, 'and I have a huge army waiting at some distance so as not to overrun your ashram. You could not possibly cater for all of us.'

'I will entertain all of you, no matter how many you are,' replied Bharadvaja. 'Bring your army here, and you will see the power of a simple hermit.'

So ordered by the sage, Bharata called for the army while Bharadvaja invoked divine spirits to help him look after them. He put forth his mystic power until powerful beings from all over the universe were invisibly assembled at that spot. Then he began to work his enchantment.

A cool breeze wafted through the trees and showers of flowers rained down from the heavens. Maidens appeared dancing to the sound of celestial music. As astonished soldiers crowded into the grove all their cares fell away. Smooth green lawns interspersed with perfumed fruit trees appeared everywhere with gardens and fountains and lovely pavilions decked with flowers and soft cushions. All imaginable kinds of delicious foods and drinks were served in unlimited quantities by beautiful women. As the men began to feast they found that no matter how much they ate they never felt full. Lovely maidens tended to their needs, taking them down to the riverside where they massaged them with scented oils and bathed them with fragrant balms. Animal carers tended the horses and elephants, grooming and feeding them until they glowed with health and satisfaction so that their keepers could no longer recognize them. The trees took on their human forms to dance and serve the guests.

Through the night feasting and revelry continued until all fell into a deep and dreamless sleep. They awoke refreshed, the fatigue and discomforts of their journey gone, to find themselves back in the forest outside Bharadvaja's ashram as if nothing had happened.

Bharata and his family took grateful leave of Bharadvaja. But before they left, the sage wanted to greet Bharata's mothers. Bharata respectfully introduced Kausalya and Sumitra, but when he came to Kaikeyi his demeanour changed.

'This is proud and cruel Kaikeyi. She is the cause of all our suffering.' His voice choked with tears of anger as he spoke.

'Do not hate Kaikeyi,' admonished the sage, 'for Rama's banishment serves a deep purpose, and will yet bring happiness to all.'

With Bharadvaja's advice ringing in his ears, Bharata set off with his army on the final march to Chitrakoot. Soldiers, chariots, horses and elephants moved through the dense forest like a monsoon cloud, scattering the deer and bears and driving squawking birds into the tree-tops. They found Chitrakoot Hill abundant with spotted deer and forest flowers. A scout called out.

'Ahead I see smoke rising among the trees. This surely is Rama's camp!'

Word reached Bharata who ordered the troops to halt while he went forward with Sumantra, the king's trusted adviser, his eyes fixed nervously on the thin blue column of smoke ahead.

ACCEPTING THE INEVITABLE

Arm in arm with Sita, Rama walked in the groves of Chitrakoot. He was happy to be here with only Sita and Lakshmana for company, and didn't in the least miss his friends and family or the burdens of state back home.

'See how lovely this mountain is. It is home to tigers and bears who will not harm us, to deer and flocks of birds. Brightly coloured flowers grow among the rocks of many hues. Mangoes, papayas, pomegranates and other fruits hang in abundance among the flowering trees. Nearby flows the Mandakini, her banks overhung with shady boughs, her waters full of swans, cranes and lotus flowers. I will happily spend my fourteen years of exile here with you, my sweetheart.'

Just then Rama became aware that something was disturbing the animals. He heard the distant trumpeting of elephants and saw a dust-cloud drifting up from the valley below.

'Lakshmana,' he called, 'what is this disturbance?'

Lakshmana scaled a tall tree and gazed to the north.

'I see an army with elephants, horses and chariots,' he shouted down. 'Put out the fire and have your bow at the ready.'

'Can you see whose army it is?' enquired Rama.

Scanning the massed ranks of men and equipment, Lakshmana made out a banner unfurled in the breeze.

'I see the white trunk and silver leaves of the emblem of Ayodhya. It must be Bharata,' he concluded, 'come to kill us both and assert his sovereignty. We will fight him,' he declared. 'He lies at the root of all your suffering and he deserves to be killed, and I shall also kill Kaikeyi. Then you can rule the world undisturbed.' As he spoke, Lakshmana's voice filled with fury.

Rama did not at all approve of Lakshmana's aggressive words and replied with equal vehemence.

'Consider what you are saying, Lakshmana. I have given my word of honour to renounce the kingdom in favour of Bharata, and now you want me to kill him and sit on a throne stained with his blood? I feel sure that Bharata has come with love in his heart, anxious to see me. But if you wish I will command him to hand over the kingdom to you. I am sure he will do it immediately.'

Corrected by his elder brother, Lakshmana felt ashamed.

'Perhaps it may be father who has come to see you,' he conceded.

'You are right, Lakshmana. He understands our trials in the forest and has come to take us home. But can you see the royal insignia of his white umbrella?' Lakshmana could not, and despondently climbed down to the ground.

Sita and Rama living in the forest, dressed in simple forest clothes of tree-bark and deerskin. Lakshmana, wearing a tiger-skin, cooks for them, while Rama, garlanded by forest flowers, looks lovingly on Sita.

Meanwhile, Bharata climbed steadily with his companions up through the trees, his eyes fixed above him on the column of smoke. Some distance behind, at a slower pace, followed Vasistha and the three queens. Bharata came to a halt. Before him the hillside levelled off and he saw in a clearing three small huts built from leafy branches. Beside them leaned shining bows and quivers, with swords and shields emblazoned with flowers of gold. In front of the huts was an altar upon which burned a sacred fire. In the midst of this scene Bharata saw his brother Rama, sitting with his hair tied in a great tangled knot and wearing a beard, his body smeared with dirt and dressed in deerskin and strips of bark. Rama, with the shoulders of a lion, looked to Bharata like Vishnu, protector of the earth. On either side of him sat Lakshmana and Sita. Choking with emotion, Bharata ran forward crying out.

'O Rama, my brother, my noble brother! What has become of you!' Rama took his younger brother in his strong arms and comforted him.

'My poor boy, you have come here without your father. I hope the emperor is in good health and has not left this world. I hope you are listening to your counsellors and governing the kingdom wisely. But tell me, dear brother, why have you left Ayodhya and come here dressed like an ascetic?'

'O Rama, do you not know? Our father has indeed left this world with a broken heart and gone to heaven. I have come to beg you to return and brighten the empire as the moon brightens the autumn sky. All of us – ministers, gurus, the entire people of Kosala – beg you to come back.'

When Rama heard of his father's death he sank to the ground.

'With father gone, what remains for me in Ayodhya? My duty is now to obey his order and live in the forest, and yours is to obey his order and rule the kingdom. Now let me pay homage to my departed father.'

Rama led Lakshmana and Sita down to the riverbank to offer water and fruits in honour of his father's spirit. Returning to the huts he clasped Bharata, Lakshmana and Satrughna and together they poured out their grief. Far below the waiting troops heard their cries, like the roaring of lions, and knew the brothers were united once more.

Bharata and Satrughna (centre) dressed in the clothes of ascetics, come in search of Rama. On the left, Lakshmana spies them from a tree-top and hurries to warn Rama.

Forest animals fled and birds flew confused into the sky. The soldiers converged from all sides, unable to bear the separation from Rama. Their faces bathed in tears, they burst into the clearing and crowded around Rama. Some fell at his feet, some embraced him, while others simply gazed on his face.

Soon Vasistha arrived with the queens. Rama touched his feet with respect. Many tears and hugs were exchanged and the company sat and talked as darkness fell.

In the morning, all settled down in a circle, full of curiosity to hear what would be said, with Rama and Bharata in the centre. Bharata began.

'Kaikeyi has now got what she wanted, though it will send her to hell. The kingdom has been given to me. I, however, cannot rule it and hereby hand it back to you.'

Rama spoke in reply, his voice clear and calm.

'As the sun rises and sets it steals away the lives of all who live. Yet we greet each new day without thinking that with it comes our death. Indeed, death is our constant

companion in this world. Therefore, I say, don't waste your tears on others, grieve for yourself, for you will die soon. We are all like pieces of driftwood floating on the ocean. Sometimes we come together, sometimes we are far apart. Our families, wealth and fortune are thus made and broken by the force of time. None of us can escape from the path already taken by our parents and grandparents, so why do we stand at the roadside to mourn their passing? Therefore my brother, do not grieve for our father, who lived a long and righteous life and has now entered the celestial world. Give up your weeping. Go home to the glorious city of Ayodhya, and I shall stay here, and together we shall do our father's bidding.' Rama fell silent.

'But your duty is not here, it is in Ayodhya,' countered Bharata. 'Let me go to the forest for fourteen years in your place.'

'You cannot stand in my place. You will be a ruler of people, I will be a ruler of wildlife.' Rama was not to be swayed from his vow. 'But after fourteen years I promise I shall return and rule the world.'

As the momentous debate went on hosts of rishis, unseen by ordinary people, gathered in the air to witness it. They wanted Rama to put an end to Ravana, so they spoke to Bharata with one voice.

'Noble prince,' they advised, 'accept Rama's advice. He must fulfil his father's obligation.' With these words they disappeared, and Bharata, realizing that he was powerless to bring Rama back, relented.

'Very well, Rama, I will return to Ayodhya without you. But still you will be our king.' He offered Rama a pair of wooden sandals. 'Place your feet on these sandals and I will install them on the throne in your absence.' Rama placed his feet on the sandals. Bharata triumphantly lifted them onto his head, announcing, 'These sandals will represent you, our king, whom I will always serve. If, however, you do not return after fourteen years, I will die by entering fire.'

'So be it!' concluded Rama. He embraced Bharata with tearful eyes.

'Forgive your mother and take care of her.'

He turned to his mothers, who were choked with tears, and said goodbye. With a long look at their beloved Rama, unshaken in his duty like the Himalaya mountains, the crowd backed away in awe. He turned and entered his cottage as the crowd melted into the trees. Inside the cottage with Sita and Lakshmana, he sat down and wept.

Bharata had done his best. Now he took Rama's words to heart. Accepting what could not be changed, he returned to Ayodhya with Rama's sandals and shed no more tears.

On reaching Ayodhya he found it darkened like a cloudy sky, its streets empty and silent. His father's chambers, where so many tragic events had occurred in the last three months, seemed like an empty cave holding the memory of a great lion who had once lived there. After bringing his mothers safely back to their quarters he made an announcement.

'I shall not live here without Rama. I will stay at the lonely retreat of Nandigram, fourteen miles from here.'

Leaving his mothers in the care of Vasistha and taking with him Satrughna and the royal army, he left for Nandigram. There he installed Rama's sandals on the throne and placed over them the royal umbrella. When affairs of state were brought to him he first submitted them before Rama in the guise of his shoes. In this way, dressed as a forest ascetic with his hair unkempt and eating only fruits and roots, Bharata governed the kingdom and waited for Rama's return.

After Bharata's visit Rama was no longer happy in Chitrakoot. It held painful memories, and the disruption caused by Bharata's army had lured man-eating demons to the area, who started disturbing the ascetics who lived there. It was rumoured that they were led by Khara, the cruel brother of Ravana. The leader of the forest sages came to warn Rama of the danger, then he and his followers left in search of safer parts. Although they left Rama, the sages never forgot his beauty and gravity, and felt his presence always with them in their hearts.

So Rama led his companions deeper into the wild regions of Dandaka Forest. Their first stop was the ashram of Atri. The sage asked Rama to protect the forest community from the rakshasas, who lived on human blood. He explained to the fearless Rama and Lakshmana where they were to be found.

Atri's wife was named Anasuya, 'one without envy', for in her heart there was no anger. Frail and white-haired after a long life of simplicity and self-denial, she gathered Sita in her arms.

'Fortunate are you,' she said, 'because your eyes are always fixed upon your husband. A woman has no greater friend than her husband. Be virtuous and devote yourself to him and you will be rewarded in heaven.'

She blessed Sita with enchanted ornaments and smeared on her skin celestial balm, so that her radiance would never fade amid the hardships of the jungle. Then she wished to hear from Sita the story of her marriage, and listened with rapt attention as Sita recounted how Rama had won her hand. While they sat together, the sun sank over the horizon.

'Listen to the cooing of the birds as they settle in their nests,' she said, 'and see the trees fading into twilight. Now the moon rises among the stars and demons of the night creep from their lairs. I wish to hear more of your sweet words but it is time for you to join your glorious husband.'

Then Sita adorned herself with Anasuya's gifts and bowed before her. Sita came before Rama shining like the moon. They spent the night in peace and departed at dawn, following the path pointed out to them by their host Atri. Rama, the scourge of his enemies, with Sita and Lakshmana, disappeared into the deep forest as the sun vanishes into a bank of clouds.

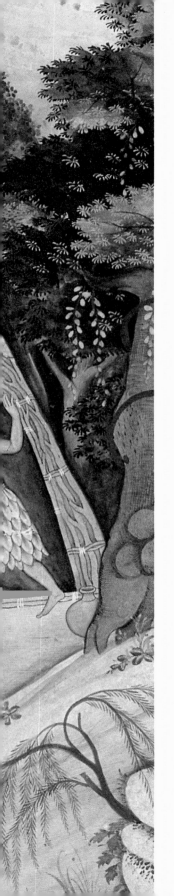

THE THIRD BOOK

Aranya Kanda

*Rama meets with disaster when Sita is kidnapped
by the demon-king Ravana. Rama searches the
empty cottage for his beloved Sita and questions the
deer for her whereabouts. In the background, Rama
and Lakshmana discover the shattered remains of
Ravana's chariot beside the dying bird Jatayu, who
fights to rescue Sita before she is carried away.*

FOREST LIFE

THE WITCH SURPANAKHA

RAMA LED THE WAY into the depths of Dandaka Forest. It seemed strangely empty of animals but filled with a dark brooding presence. They saw signs of destruction, such as trees stripped of their branches and the remains of animals brutally mutilated. Suddenly from the shadows emerged a huge deformed creature dressed in tiger skins, dragging behind it several animal carcasses. It pounced on Sita and carried her off.

'My name is Viradha,' it roared, 'and I will keep this woman.' Rama hesitated at what to do. The demon saw that they were not ordinary ascetics and demanded to know who they were. Rama told him their names and shot seven arrows into the body of Viradha. In fury the demon released Sita and charged upon the two brothers. They rained arrows upon him, but he merely laughed and shrugged them off.

'No weapon can hurt me. I was once a celestial being, but am now cursed to live as a man-eater. Only Rama, the son of Dasaratha, can free me. Now, Rama, you are here, so please kill me and release me from this curse.' He told Rama to bury him alive, as this was the only way he could be killed. So they dug a deep pit and buried Viradha. With his last breath he murmured:

'Forgive me, lord, I did not recognize you. This forest is a dangerous place. Go to the sage Sarabhanga on the nearby hill and he will advise where you can safely stay.'

Following Viradha's counsel they made their way to the ashram of Sarabhanga. As they approached it they saw a golden chariot, yolked with four green horses, hovering in the air above the place. In it sat Indra, king of heaven, but as soon as he saw them he rose swiftly into the sky. Sarabhanga came out to greet them, saying:

'Indra is here to take me to heaven as a reward for my austerities. But first I have waited to see you, my Lord. I must advise you to see Sutikishna. Follow the course of the Mandakini river and you will find his ashram. He will show you your way in the forest. Now, having seen you, I can go to paradise.' Then before their eyes, the old sage was transformed into a dazzling youth and was raised up into the heavens.

They were about to leave when a throng of sages emerged from the forest to petition Rama. 'This region is terrorized by man-eating demons,' they cried. 'Please

Rama and Sita engage in spiritual discussions with forest sages.

The witch Surpanakha, spurned by Rama and Lakshmana, tries to attack Sita, whereupon Lakshmana uses his arrows to cut off her nose and ears.

fight them or we will all be killed.' Rama promised them his protection. Sita, however, was against fighting. She wanted him to live in the forest without violence.

They moved steadily south-west across the Deccan plateau, coming to Sutikishna's ashram, on the peak of a mountain. He advised them to travel through the region visiting the ashrams of saintly hermits. They did this and wherever they went were ample fruits and roots, herds of deer and crystal-clear lakes. Continuing westwards they reached the ashram of the sage Agastya. His strength kept that part of the forest free from demons. He received them with due honour and presented Rama with a set of divine weapons, once used by Vishnu.

'Tell us where we should stay,' asked Rama.

'Two days' walk from here is the beautiful forest of Panchavati,' replied the sage, 'always full of blossoms and close beside the river Godaveri. There you must defend the sages from the attack of rakshasas.' Agastya's directions were clear, and resolved any doubts: using Vishnu's weapons, Rama must fight to defend the sages.

So they journeyed to Panchavati, following the path pointed out to them by Agastya until they reached the foot of the mountains of the Western Ghats. As they entered the region they encountered a gigantic and terrifying vulture. At first they took it for another demon ready to devour them, until Rama asked who it was. It replied:

'Dear son, I am a friend of your father. My name is Jatayu and I am nephew of

Garuda, the divine carrier of Vishnu. I will protect Sita from the demons who live here.' Rama was grateful for this offer, and together they entered Panchavati.

Lakshmana built a cottage of earth, bamboo and thatch for Sita and Rama, and covered its floor with reed matting. As winter set in, a cold westerly wind blew and the woodlands were wrapped in fog. Mist shrouded the river and elephants shrank from its touch. Still the brothers and the princess bathed each morning in the cold waters and offered prayers through the mists to the rising sun.

One morning they were surprised to see a strange misshapen creature, half woman, half monster. Her skin was rough and her face and body ugly. She gazed on Rama, infatuated with his beauty, and spoke with a rasping voice:

'Noble creature, who are you and what are you doing here?'

'I am Rama, son of Dasaratha,' said Rama politely. 'This is Lakshmana, my younger brother, and here is Sita my wife. We are here on the command of my father to do penance. But tell me, charming lady of slender limb, who are you and what brings you to our cottage?'

'My name is Surpanakha, sister of the demon-king Ravana,' she replied, her passions inflamed by Rama's gallant words. 'I live near here with my two cousins, Khara and Dusana. Ever since I first saw you I have wanted you. I am not feeble like this ugly Sita – I have strength and passion equal to yours. Let me devour Sita and Lakshmana so that we can be alone in the forest!'

'But I am already married,' laughed Rama. 'Why don't you choose Lakshmana, my younger brother? He is handsome and strong and would make a far better husband for you.' Hearing this, Surpanakha turned her amorous attentions upon Lakshmana.

'Come then, Lakshmana, I will be your wife and we will wander through the forest together.'

'But why should you want me, O beauty of soft complexion,' joked Lakshmana, 'when I am merely the servant of Rama? Better that you become Rama's wife, and replace this ugly Sita.'

Surpanakha's simple brain was confused. She knew only that Sita stood in her way. With eyes like red-hot coals she rushed at Sita, intent on killing her.

'Punish her, Lakshmana!' cried Rama, catching hold of the hideous monster. In an instant Lakshmana had cut off her ears and her nose, making her roar in agony. The unfortunate creature, splattered in blood, fled deep into the jungle.

Surpanakha flew straight to her cousin Khara and threw herself on the ground in front of him, bleeding and sobbing. He was shocked to see her condition and said, 'My poor cousin, what fool has done this to you, inviting instant death?'

'Two handsome princes, Rama and Lakshmana, dressed as ascetics, are in the forest with a beautiful young girl. Out of jealousy she made them do this to me. I will not be satisfied until you have killed them all and I have drunk the girl's blood.'

Khara, in fury, dispatched fourteen rakshasa demons from his personal guard to kill Rama and his companions. Surpanakha led them to the cottage. Seeing them, Rama quickly ordered Lakshmana to take Sita away to a safe distance, leaving him to deal with the intruders alone.

The rakshasas charged at Rama, hurling spears and clubs, but he cut down their projectiles with fourteen gold-tipped arrows. He then shot another fourteen arrows, killing each of the rakshasas. Surpanakha, pale and shaken, escaped and hurried back to her cousin.

'I have sent my soldiers to avenge you,' growled Khara, 'so why are you now rolling on the ground like a wounded serpent?'

'I have seen a terrible thing,' wailed Surpanakha. 'Those brave demons of yours have all been slain by Rama. He killed them as easily as a lion kills jackals, and now I am afraid. This Rama has entered our forest with his sharp arrows and I don't see how you can stand up to him. We will all be killed. What are you going to do?'

'Stop your tears, cousin,' assured Khara, biting his lip in rage. 'Today I will send Rama to the abode of death.'

Khara ordered his brother Dusana to bring an army of fourteen-thousand rakshasas. He ascended his golden chariot, engraved with alligators, moons and stars, with wheels encrusted with jewels, and hung about with bells. Looking like Death personified, he rode through the jungle with his dreaded army, bristling with clubs, spears, javelins, swords, axes and scimitars. On his way his left arm throbbed and his eyes dimmed with tears. He saw a red halo around the sun, and darkness enveloped him even though it was daytime. His horses slipped on the road, and a vulture perched upon his flagpole.

'What do I care for these bad omens?' shrieked Khara. 'Nothing can stand in my way.' He encouraged his army to go forward with a great battle roar.

Rama, meanwhile, experienced good omens: his right arm throbbed, favourable birds perched on nearby branches and Lakshmana's face shone brightly. At the approach of the demon army he ordered Lakshmana to take Sita to a safe place. Divine beings gathered anxiously in the sky to watch.

The ensigns of the demons came into view with much shouting and clashing of swords on shields. Rama stood alone, holding his bow tightly before him, his knuckles white, eyes pin-pointed on the approaching enemy, his arrows at the ready. His usually gentle face was suffused with anger, and he shone like a white-hot flame.

Khara surrounded Rama with his troops. Thousands of weapons of all description rained down on the solitary hero. Rama was besieged like a mountain peak enveloped in storm clouds, but he stood firm and poured arrows from his bow, intercepting the incoming weapons and absorbing their fury as the ocean absorbs a river in flood. His bow seemed permanently bent in a great arc as his arrows struck the hearts of the demons. He split their bows, cut their ensigns and destroyed their chariots, driving them back to Khara for protection.

Dusana, Khara's brother and general, rallied the demons and led a fresh assault. Arrows, clubs, uprooted trees and boulders fell on Rama from all sides. He invoked a celestial weapon which threw back the entire host. His hands did not appear to move, only to rest on his bowstring, yet thousands of razor-sharp arrows streamed from his bow, hiding the sun. Rama gradually reduced the demons until the ground was strewn thickly with helmets, broken weapons and broken bodies. Out of this carnage rushed Dusana, armed with an enormous gold-plated club spiked with iron, capable of flattening a whole army, but Rama's arrows cut off his arms and killed him.

Trisira, Khara's greatest champion, terrible to look upon with three heads, advanced like a black storm-cloud emitting torrents of arrows and roaring like thunder. He clashed with Rama as a lion clashes with an elephant, wounding him on the forehead. Enraged, Rama released arrows, destroying his chariot and cutting off his three heads. Blood spurted from his severed trunk as he fell dead, and his cohorts fled terrified into the forest.

Now it was Khara's turn. With fear in his heart he discharged magical weapons into the sky and charged at Rama as a moth is drawn into a fire. He pierced Rama with many arrows and split his bow, but Rama felt the arrows as an elephant feels the striking of a goad. He took up the diamond-studded bow of Vishnu given to him by Agastya and released nineteen deadly shafts. Six pierced Khara's head, arms and chest, twelve shattered his chariot and killed his chariot driver and horses, and one struck him in the heart, knocking him to the ground.

'You have persecuted holy men of the forest for mere sport,' said Rama. 'Now reap the reward of your sinful deeds. The sages you killed are watching this fight from the sky. Now they will see you dispatched to hell.'

But Khara stood firm with his huge mace.

'What is the use of your boastful words, when I am about to kill you?' he retorted. 'I believe in action, not boastful words. You have killed all my soldiers, but now I will wipe away the tears of their relatives.' Then he hurled his mace, which blazed with fire and burned the surrounding forest to ashes. As it flew through the air towards him, Rama shattered it into a thousand fragments with his arrows. The demon uprooted a big tree, whirled it above his head and threw it at Rama, but Rama's arrows cut the tree to pieces. Filled with anger, he pierced Khara with countless arrow shafts. Maddened by the smell of his own blood, the demon summoned his last strength to run headlong at Rama. Using a special arrow given to him by Agastya and the bow of Vishnu, Rama struck Khara in the chest. The smoking arrow entered the demon's heart with a sound like thunder, killing him instantly.

The divine beings in the sky praised Rama and showered him with flowers. Sita emerged from hiding with Lakshmana to embrace him in relief and joy. The forest was safe once more.

EVIL RAVANA

Ten-headed Ravana shifted uneasily on his throne. His twenty arms and broad chest were covered with scars from countless battles with the gods, any one of which would have killed a lesser being. He listened as Akampana, the sole survivor of Khara's army, told him how a mere man had single-handedly killed his entire garrison in Dandaka forest. His eyes burned blood-red and he hissed like a cobra.

'Who is this man to risk my wrath?' asked Ravana.

'He is the glorious Rama, son of Dasaratha,' replied Akampana.

'Then I shall go myself and destroy him.' replied Ravana.

'I would not advise it, O mighty king, said Akampana. 'Rama is invincible; his arrows can bring down the very stars from the sky. But he has one weakness: his beautiful wife Sita. Without her he will lose his will to live.'

'Then I shall carry her off in my chariot,' retorted Ravana.

Mounting his golden chariot inlaid with jewels and drawn by mules, Ravana flew to his magician friend Maricha's distant hermitage. But when Maricha heard Ravana's intention he advised him against it.

'What fool has advised you to kidnap Sita?' he asked. 'It would be better to drink poison.' So for a while Ravana swallowed his anger and desisted from his plan.

Then his sister Surpanakha, her face scarred, came to him eager for revenge.

'I have been disfigured, your territory has been usurped and fourteen thousand of your soldiers killed while you idly enjoy yourself. What kind of ruler are you?' she taunted, and again Ravana's anger was stirred.

'Tell me of this Rama,' he said. 'What is his strength? How does he fight? Is it he who has disfigured you?'

'Rama is handsome like the god of love, but his arrows bite like serpents,' replied Surpanakha. 'I could not see when he took arrows from his quiver, when he bent his bow or when he released them. I could only see our soldiers fall like a field of corn before a hailstorm. In an hour and a half he killed fourteen thousand of them. His brother Lakshmana did this atrocity to me on account of Sita, his beautiful wife. She presides over the forest like a goddess, and her beauty surpasses the whole creation. She is a worthy consort for you. Take her for your own, and be avenged on Rama!'

In his fury, Ravana again approached Maricha for help in kidnapping Sita. But Maricha had his own reasons to fear Rama and tried to dissuade him.

'You underestimate Rama's strength,' he replied, full of dread. 'You will never succeed in taking Sita, any more than you could steal the brilliance from the sun, but if somehow you do Rama will surely kill you in battle and lay waste to the city of Lanka.'

'I did not ask your opinion,' Ravana replied sharply, 'I merely asked your help. Go to Dandaka Forest and use your magical art to take the shape of a golden deer. Show yourself to Sita, who will surely ask Rama to catch you, then while he is away mimic his voice to call Lakshmana. While Sita is unprotected I will capture her.'

'Forget Sita, or you condemn us both to death with this perilous plan,' Maricha rasped, his mouth dry with fear.

'Do as I ask, or fail me and your life is worth nothing. I do not keep traitors. Risk death from Rama, or face certain death from me. The choice is yours.'

'Very well. I will accept death from Rama, which will be better than death from you. But I warn you, when he has killed me he will come for you and destroy your kingdom. But you will not heed my words – a person who is destined to die does not accept advice from friends.'

'Then let us leave,' pronounced Ravana, and together they boarded his chariot and sped to Dandaka Forest.

A cave-painting of Ravana, the demon-king of Lanka.

RAVANA

RAVANA was the celebrated demon-king of Lanka. His original name was Dasagriva, meaning ten heads; Ravana means 'one who makes others cry'. He earned this name attempting to move Mount Kailas, where Shiva was consorting with his wife. Shiva steadied the mountain, trapping Ravana who shouted for his life. Ravana's desire for distinction was so great that he sat in penance for ten thousand years. Finally, Brahma granted him the boon of invulnerability against gods and demons.

Although in *Ramayana* Ravana is portrayed as savage and cruel, there are those who worship him. Even Rama himself is quoted as saying at his death that Ravana was a gifted and courageous character who deserved to be buried with reverence.

THE GOLDEN DEER

Sita had gone a little way from the cottage to collect flowers, when she caught sight of a beautiful golden deer among the trees. It was unlike any she had seen before, with horns glinting like sapphire, hoofs like gems and golden flanks spotted with silver. It pranced and spun in circles, then cocked its head to gaze at her. She was captivated.

'Rama, Lakshmana, do look!'

The brothers saw the deer, but Lakshmana, ever vigilant, was suspicious.

'Beware, Rama, this is no real deer – it is an illusion of the demon Maricha, who practices this deception to lure his prey. He has killed and eaten many this way.'

'But it is so beautiful,' said Sita. 'Do catch it for me, my lord, and we can keep it as a pet. Or you could kill it and we will sit on its golden skin.'

'You will have this deer, alive or dead,' promised Rama. 'If, as Lakshmana says, it turns out to be Maricha I will slay him just as he has slain so many.'

Rama made Lakshmana stay with Sita to protect her, then took up his bow in pursuit of the deer. He tried to capture it but it fled deep into the forest, luring him far from the cottage. Growing uneasy he decided to kill it, and sent a flaming arrow into its heart. Struck to the core and on the point of dying, Maricha shed the illusory shape of the golden deer and revealed his true monstrous form. In agony he cried out, mimicking Rama's voice, 'Alas Sita! Lakshmana, help me!' and gave up his life.

The forest fell silent. Rama felt his heart grow cold with fear for Sita. He sped back in the direction of the cottage.

Sita and Lakshmana had heard the plaintive cry, and Sita appealed to him to go and help Rama, but he did not stir.

'Why don't you go?'

'Princess, there is no need. Your husband is invincible and no one, demon or god, can harm him. What you heard was not Rama's voice, but a trick of Maricha. Rama has ordered me to protect you and I cannot leave you here alone.'

'Are you Rama's enemy, that you want him to die so that you can possess me?' cried Sita in outrage. 'Is it me you have wanted all this time? You deceitful and cruel man!'

Her words cut Lakshmana to the quick.

'Very well, I will go to Rama,' he spoke in anger and hurt, 'but you are in grave danger. May the woodland deities protect you!' And he was gone, leaving Sita streaming tears and beating her breast.

As night follows day, the coming of Ravana followed Lakshmana's departure. Disguised in the saffron robes of an ascetic, he advanced through the trees towards the cottage. As he did so the birds fell silent and the air went still. He saw Sita on the ground in front of her cottage, her moonlike face bathed in tears, and he was smitten by the arrow of love.

'O delicate lady, I am enchanted by your slender waist, broad hips and round breasts. I have never seen such loveliness. Who are you and why are you alone in this dangerous forest?'

Confused and afraid, Sita did her best to receive the mendicant with due respect, offering him a seat and giving him food and water. As she did so she looked around nervously for Rama or Lakshmana, but saw only the dense green forest spread in all directions. She introduced herself, then asked who he was. His answer terrified her.

'I am ten-headed Ravana, feared by all the gods. My capital, across the sea, is Lanka, the most beautiful and best fortified city in the universe. Come and live there with me, where five thousand maids will serve you. Forget Rama. He is not even equal to my little finger.'

'I am the devoted wife of Rama,' protested Sita, 'who is a lion among men. Beside him you are a jackal, and can never hope to have me.' Her body shook with fear. 'You may think yourself invincible, but if you take me your life is at an end!'

Bristling with anger, Ravana showed his true colossal form, with ten heads, blood-red eyes, and twenty arms, covered in red robes and golden ornaments. Grasping Sita's hair he dragged her to his golden chariot.

'O Rama, you do not know what is happening to me!' Sita cried as Ravana's chariot rose into the sky. 'O trees, rivers and spirits of the forest, all you animals and birds, please tell my dearest Rama that Sita was carried away by Ravana.'

All this time Jatayu slept in a nearby tree. Now the bird awoke to see a tragedy unfolding. He spread his wings and took to the air, warning Ravana.

'Old as I am, I will kill you as Rama killed your brother. Stay and fight with me, prowler of the night!'

Ravana turned on Jatayu, like one mountain clashing with another, and struck him with hundreds of barbed arrows. Jatayu tore at him with his sharp talons and beak, breaking his bow, killing his mules and chariot driver, and sending his chariot crashing down to the ground.

Ravana held Sita tightly as he fell to the ground. Then, leaving her, he rose once more into the sky by mystic power alone. Jatayu swooped upon his back and slashed at his head and shoulders, tearing off his twenty arms. But as each arm was lost,

Rama pursues the magical golden deer deep into Dandaka Forest. He recognizes it as an illusion created by the magician-demon Maricha to lure away Sita, and finally Rama decides to kill it with a flaming arrow.

Leaving Lakshmana to guard Sita at the cottage, Rama goes in pursuit of the magical golden deer, which proves to be the demon Maricha.

another one grew in its place. The aged Jatayu grew tired while Ravana's fury intensified. He severed Jatayu's wings, and he fell to the ground, able to rise no more.

Sita cried bitterly and embraced Jatayu as he lay dying. She tried to flee but, laughing, the cruel monster took her by the hair a second time and lifted her up into the darkening sky.

In the heavens the gods watched. 'Our purpose is accomplished,' they said grimly. 'His destruction is now certain. Nothing can save him from the wrath of Rama.'

Ravana carried Sita through the air to Lanka, like a cloud flashing with lightning.

'You shameless creature!' she cried. 'My lord will pursue you to the ends of the earth, and once he has found you your life will not last one hour. You are caught in the noose of death!'

As Ravana's shadow sped over the forests, Sita spied far below five great monkey chiefs seated on a mountain peak. She tied her jewels in her silk wrapper and threw them down, unnoticed by Ravana. The monkey chiefs received the jewels and looked up with unwinking eyes. They saw Sita, her face wet with tears, coursing through the air in the grip of Ravana. Unaware that he had been seen, the evil monster flew on to Lanka, carrying in his arms his own death in the form of Sita.

THE EMPTY COTTAGE

Rama had gone further from the cottage than he intended. As he hurried back, deep in the jungle behind him a jackal gave forth a lonely howl, sending a shiver down his spine. He knew the rakshasas would want revenge for the terrible defeat he had inflicted on them. Now, with Maricha's trick unmasked, he feared the worst. How could he have been fooled so easily? His only hope was that Lakshmana had not been taken in

While the cottage is unattended, demon-king Ravana advances on Sita, disguised in the saffron robes of an ascetic.

As ten-headed Ravana carries Sita through the sky, the mighty vulture Jatayu attacks him in an attempt to rescue Sita.

by Maricha's false cry for help and had stayed with Sita. Yet his worst fears were confirmed when he met Lakshmana coming alone the other way, his face ashen.

'Where is Sita?' Rama called out in dismay. 'I fear that some demon will have carried her away or killed her.' Lakshmana, realizing his mistake, remained silent.

'Where is she who shared my sufferings with me all this time?' Rama continued. 'Is she still alive? If not, I shall die.'

Racing through the undergrowth, scratched and bruised, they came to the cottage. All was empty and silent, mats and eating utensils in disarray. The only sound was the trees creaking in the wind.

'Why did you leave her?' cried Rama. Lakshmana sorrowfully tried to explain what had happened.

'You should not have taken a woman's harsh words so seriously,' Rama reproached, then pondered, 'perhaps she has gone to the river to fetch water, or out to gather flowers.' They looked in her favourite places, but could not find her. Running here and there like a madman, Rama scoured the forest calling out to the trees and animals.

'Trees, did my dear Sita come to you gathering flowers? Deer, did she pass this way? Tigers, did you see her moonlike face?' He imagined he saw her before him. 'Why are you running away from me, my darling? Wait, come back!' He returned to the empty cottage and called out, 'Come out now, sweetheart, do not jest. I know you are hiding. Please do not leave me – I can't live without you.'

'Don't give in to this madness, brother,' said Lakshmana. 'We must try to find her. She may have wandered off, so we shall search the mountains, caves, rivers and forests.' But although they searched long, no trace of Sita could be found. Lakshmana tried his best to console his brother, but Rama cried bitter tears.

'How will I ever be able to return to Ayodhya without Sita? Lakshmana, you must go back and tell them that without Sita I could not live. Tell Bharata to take the throne and rule the earth. My sinful deeds in past births have now caught up with me. She has been taken by cruel demons who even now drink her blood. To think that she used to sit here on this rock with me. I can hear her laughter still. O Wind god, you know everything. Did you see which way she went?'

'Please take heart,' reassured Lakshmana. 'It's no good crying like this, Rama. We must find Sita, not simply cry for her.' But Rama was lost in an ocean of grief and could not heed him.

Rama asked the deer for news of Sita, whereupon they all looked up to the sky and turned their heads south, walking slowly in that direction, looking first to the sky then to the ground. Lakshmana read their movements and called Rama to follow. Soon they found signs of Sita's abduction: flowers from her hair scattered on the ground, huge rakshasa footprints and beside them Sita's footprints running away, then the shattered remains of a golden chariot, with quivers and a broken bow encrusted with gems lying close by. Then they found evidence of a fierce fight with drops of blood strewn about. Nearby they found the gigantic crushed bodies of mules and a dead charioteer still grasping his reins and whip.

'Where is she?' shouted Rama angrily, his eyes burning and his lips trembling. 'If the gods do not return her, I will throw them from heaven and annihilate the world with my arrows.'

Unable to bear Rama's agony, Lakshmana stood before him with joined hands.

'My lord, you are not yourself. I know you to be mild like the moon and patient like the earth. Come back to your true self. With me as your companion and sages as your helpers, you will find Sita. We will search the oceans and rivers, forests and mountains until we find her. We will leave no place untouched. If after that we do not find her then you may annihilate the worlds. Take heart – everyone in this world must accept sorrow and pain and learn to overcome them. You are strong enough to be steady in the face of this calamity. Show your true qualities and awaken your wisdom. Let us take decisive action!'

Rama accepted his younger brother's good instruction. Controlling his anger and leaning on his mighty bow, he recovered himself.

'What shall we do then, good brother?'

'Let us first search the entire region: gorges, chasms, valleys and caves – all the places loved by demons – then consider what else to do.'

They set off, bows in hand. Almost immediately they found Jatayu, lying on the ground like a fallen mountain. Rama took him for a demon and was about to finish him with an arrow, when he heard him murmur: 'O child, the lady you seek was carried off by a great rakshasa, along with my life. I tried to stop him, but he got the best of me. I killed his charioteer and destroyed his chariot, but now he has flown to the south with Sita.'

'Who was he,' asked Rama desperately, seeing Jatayu's life ebbing fast, 'and where did he take her?'

'It was the evil Ravana, the half-brother of Kuvera,' whispered Jatayu, his voice fading.

'Speak more!' begged Rama, but Jatayu had breathed his last.

'This king of the birds was a great soul, Lakshmana, who sacrificed his life for my service,' said Rama. 'Souls such as this can be found even among birds and animals. He was my devoted servant and his passing pains me as much as the loss of Sita. Fetch some wood so that we may give him a worthy cremation, and help him attain the reward for his great sacrifice.'

They burned Jatayu's remains and chanted prayers over them. After bathing in the river, they offered fruits in his memory and found peace in their minds. They then put that place, and its memories, behind them and set off to the south in search of Sita.

Rama and Lakshmana search everywhere for Sita; they come upon the dying Jatayu; after Jatayu's death, in the far distance, they cremate him by the riverside and offer fruits in his memory.

THE SEARCH BEGINS

At first Rama and Lakshmana were confronted with densely tangled jungle. With great difficulty they managed to penetrate it and find a way to the west, out of Dandaka Forest. They entered another forest, filled with a threatening presence. Lakshmana's left arm throbbed and he felt a sense of foreboding. They heard from the heart of the forest a terrible roar. With swords drawn they went towards it, and found a strange and horrifying monster of awesome dimensions.

The creature was blue and covered in bristling hairs, without head or legs, but with two enormous arms. In the centre of its body was a large mouth filled with sharp teeth above which blazed a single eye. Rama and Lakshmana surveyed it from a good distance, but without approaching them it suddenly extended its great arms across the intervening space and seized them, squeezing the breath from their bodies.

Caught in its grip, they thought that now, after having survived so many calamities, their end had at last come. But as the monster carried them towards its mouth to swallow them they were able to draw their swords and each sever an arm at the shoulder, rendering it powerless. It spoke to them.

'Who are you two heroes that have so fearlessly overcome me?'

'This is Rama, son of Emperor Dasaratha, and I am Lakshmana his brother. Rama has been exiled to the forest by his father and now seeks Sita, his consort, who was carried away by a rakshasa. But who are you and how did you get this terrible form?'

'I will tell you my story,' said the monster. 'I was once Kabandha, a demigod of the heavens, equal in beauty to the Sun god himself. For my amusement I used to terrorize the rishis of the forest in this monstrous form. One day I assailed a powerful mystic who cursed me to be trapped in this body. I begged him for mercy and he conceded that when Lord Rama would come and cremate me in a lonely forest I would regain my former splendour. Since then I have stayed here in this forest and made it my habit to grab anything that moves in the hope that one day this Rama would fall into my grasp. Now, Lord Rama, you have come to save me and I await your mercy. If you do what must be done by burning this body to ashes, I will regain my godly form as well as the ability to give you good advice for your search.'

Rama and Lakshmana readily agreed to help the ogre, and asked for help in return.

'We know that Sita was taken by the rakshasa king Ravana, but we do not know what he looks like or where he lives. Help us in this.'

They gathered together wood and built a fire and placed the monster upon it. As its ugly body sizzled and melted into the flames, the celestial Kabandha emerged, brilliant and joyful, decorated with gorgeous robes and ornaments and garlanded with unfading flowers. An aerial chariot appeared before him and he seated himself upon it, illuminating all directions with his effulgence, and then turned to Rama.

'Listen to my advice,' he said. 'It is said that a person suffering misfortune should make alliance with another suffering similar misfortune. There is a monkey chief called Sugriva, who was cast out of his kingdom by his brother Vali. He is a great hero, being the son of Surya, the Sun god. He will help you in your quest for Sita. I tell you this: his monkeys will search every corner and whether she is on the pinnacle of heaven or in the depths of the underworld, they will find her, and restore her to you after helping you destroy the demon Ravana and his armies.'

'You will find Sugriva by the side of Pampa lake. From here you must go westwards passing through forests of abundant fruit trees. You will see places resembling paradise, with dripping honey and nectar-like fruits. Pass over mountain and hill until you reach the lotus-filled lake of Pampa. There you will find the ashram of the saintly woman Sabari, who even now awaits your arrival. After visiting her, look for Sugriva on Rishyamukha Hill, to the east of the lake.' Even as he spoke, Kabandha began to glow, rising into the heavens, calling, 'Seek Sugriva!' and was gone.

Following the way pointed out to them, the brothers reached the edge of Pampa and there they saw the hermitage of Sabari. She clasped their feet in joy.

'I have kept for you many forest foods, please come to my ashram,' she begged. 'Today my life of penance is at an end. I have seen you, Lord Rama, who are the greatest of the gods and the flower of humanity. I shall now depart this world in peace.' At their request she showed them round the ashram, which had been home to Matanga and other great sadhus who had already departed this world for the supreme destination.

'Now, lord, permit me to cast off this aged body, long worn out by practice of penance and prayer. I long to join those great souls who went before me, and whom I served with love.' Before their eyes she entered a mystic fire and was transformed, emerging in an ethereal form which vanished up into the sky.

'By the company of this saintly woman,' said Rama, 'I feel thoroughly purified. Whatever bad karma we have been suffering has been cleansed, and now our good fortune awaits us, beginning with our meeting with Sugriva.'

Meanwhile, carrying in his arms his death incarnate, Ravana reached the city of Lanka. He handed Sita to rakshasa women, telling them to serve her every need. Next he sent eight of his most powerful warriors to Dandaka Forest as spies to keep him informed of Rama's movements. His mind turned to Sita and how to win her love. He showed her his palace housing thousands of women, with pillars of ivory and crystal, stairways of gold, walls studded with diamonds and floors inlaid with gems.

'The city of Lanka covers eight hundred square miles and is impregnable,' he boasted. 'I command two hundred million rakshasas. All this I give, if you will be my queen.'

'Further, I give you Puspaka, the magical space-ship I won from my half-brother Kuvera, the treasurer of the gods. It will take us anywhere you wish to go with the speed of thought. But come, dear lady, why look so miserable?'

Sita's face was wet with tears. 'You have unlawfully kidnapped me, you evil monster, and your death is sealed. You can keep me in chains or put me to death – I will never give myself to you.'

'I will give you one year to surrender to me,' growled Ravana. 'After that, my sweet, I will have you cut into pieces and served for my breakfast.' He called the rakshasa women. 'Take her to the ashok grove and hold her captive there. Give her no rest, but torment her until she agrees to surrender to me.'

Sita, thinking only of her lord, fainted and was carried away.

THE FOUR ASHRAMS

*The marriage procession of Rama and Sita. Marriage is the second stage in
the journey of life for all Hindus. A Hindu wife is enjoined to look upon her
husband as her guru, while he is to look upon her as a goddess.*

JUST AS THERE are four classes, or
varnas, in Hindu society, so there
are four stages of life, called ashrams.

The first is the stage of student life,
called brahmacari, when students
practice celibacy and study under the
guidance of a guru.

Secondly, the duty of all men and
women is to marry and establish a
household, called grihastha ashram.
The ideal during this stage is that the
husband gives maintenance and protection to his wife while she gives him
her devotion and service.

The next stage, called varnaprastha,
comes when the children are grown up
and the husband and wife retire to go
on pilgrimage and devote themselves to
the service of God and their community.

The final ashram is when husband
and wife voluntarily separate for the
last years of their life and the husband
takes the vow of sannyasa, or total
celibacy, after which he depends on
alms and lives alone to meditate or
travels to teach others on the spiritual
path, leaving his wife dependent upon
her sons for support and protection.

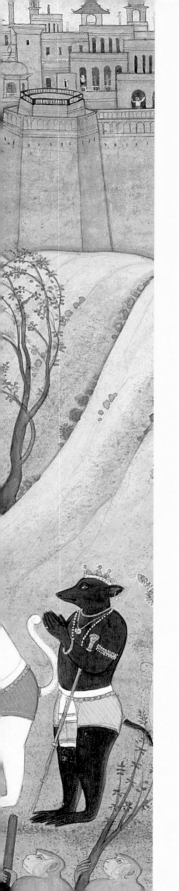

THE FOURTH BOOK

Kiskindha Kanda

While searching for Sita, Rama meets with Sugriva and makes a crucial alliance with him. Rama helps him to become the leader of the monkeys and in return, Sugriva assembles a vast monkey army to find and rescue Sita. Rama gives instructions to the monkey lord Sugriva and to Jambavan, lord of the bears. The monkeys and bears carry their characteristic weapons: rocks and uprooted trees.

THE MONKEY KINGDOM

ALLIANCE WITH THE MONKEYS

 ESIDE PAMPA LAKE THE season of spring had carpeted the soft turf with blue and yellow flowers, covered the trees and creepers in blossom, and wafted black honeybees among the perfumed blooms. Creepers embraced the trees like amorous young women with their lovers, cuckoos sang love-songs and peacocks danced.

Rama could think only of Sita. The lotus flowers on the lake reminded him of her; he heard her calling him to see the beauty of the waterfalls and smelled her in the scented flowers. Without her, he could not live.

'Perhaps she will give up her life when she sees spring without me,' he spoke aloud. 'If she would come to me now, I would be satisfied here forever, and would never wish again for Ayodhya or even the pleasures of paradise.'

'Be patient,' said Lakshmana. 'Now is the time for heroism and determination, not grief and despondency. We must find her wherever Ravana has hidden her.'

One day Sugriva, lord of the monkey tribes called the Vanaras, came near the lake to gather fruits and spied them. When he saw those two mighty princes he froze in fear, thinking them allies of his enemy Vali. He hurried back to his lair and called together his counsellors.

'Vali has sent two powerful warriors, disguised as hermits. How shall we protect ourselves?' Among his followers was Hanuman, son of the Wind god, who was wise and fearless. He counselled Sugriva.

'We need not fear Vali, who cannot enter this region. Why should we panic at the sight of two men?'

'These are no ordinary men,' replied Sugriva. 'They look more like gods, and they may be with Vali. Go and observe them closely and find out their business.'

Hanuman disguised himself as a forest hermit and approached the two brothers. Bowing before them, he spoke with gentle words.

'I salute you. With eyes like lotuses and weapons of gold you look like the Moon god and Sun god. I am Hanuman, son of the Wind god, minister of the monkey-lord Sugriva. Pray tell me who you are and what brings you here.'

Hanuman's words showed him to be learned and gentle, and Rama answered him with respect. 'I am Rama, son of Dasaratha, and this is my brother Lakshmana.' He went on to say how they came to be in the forest, and how Sita had been kidnapped. 'We know of Sugriva and we seek his friendship and help,' said Lakshmana.

Hanuman thought these two men would be valuable allies for Sugriva. He in turn told them how Sugriva had been exiled and how he had lost his wife at the hands of his cruel brother Vali. 'Come, I will take you to Sugriva,' he concluded. Revealing his true monkey form, he lifted the brothers onto his shoulders and carried them through the forest to Sugriva's camp on Rishyamukha Hill. Arriving among Sugriva's assembly, Hanuman introduced Rama and explained that he needed help.

'I am indeed fortunate,' said Sugriva, rising to greet Rama. 'Here is my hand in token of my friendship, if you will accept it.' Rama gladly clasped Sugriva's hand and warmly embraced him. Then Hanuman lit a fire between the two and together they walked around it to seal their alliance.

'We are now united as friends, and our joys and sorrows are one,' declared Sugriva, hugely satisfied. Breaking off a large leafy branch from a nearby tree he offered it to Rama as a seat and sat beside him, while Hanuman did the same, breaking another branch and sharing it with Lakshmana. Sugriva then confided in Rama.

'I live in fear of my brother Vali. Please protect me.'

'Don't worry,' reassured Rama. 'You have my word that I shall kill this Vali and help you recover your wife.'

'I have some news for you about Sita,' spoke Sugriva. 'I was sitting with four friends on top of the hill some days ago when we saw a strange sight. Passing over us in the air was a princess struggling in the arms of Ravana. As they flew above us she threw down a wrapper containing shining jewels.' He showed Rama the jewels. Instantly recognizing them, Rama could not hold back his tears, and cried, 'My darling!' holding them to his heart.

'Tell me where Ravana has taken her and I will send him to his death this very day,' he swore.

Rama and Lakshmana sit on leafy branches with their new ally Sugriva, who shows them Sita's jewels wrapped in a silk cloth.

85

'I do not know where Ravana lives or where he has taken Sita,' confessed Sugriva, 'but I give you my word that I and my monkeys will find her. Do not give way to this overwhelming grief. As your friend I beg you to be manful and restrain your tears.'

'I am thankful for your words of advice,' said Rama. 'You are a true friend in time of need. But tell me, how can I help you?'

Sugriva told Rama his story. Vali, his elder brother, son of Indra the Rain god, was ruler of the Vanara kingdom of Kiskindha. One day the demon Mayavi challenged Vali to a duel. Taking Sugriva with him, Vali went to face him, but the demon fled. They gave chase, and Mayavi hid in a deep cave. Ordering his brother to stand guard outside the cave, Vali went in after him. A year passed and still he had not returned, so Sugriva, thinking his brother dead, sealed the mouth of the cave with a large stone and returned to Kiskindha, where he was crowned king in Vali's place. Meanwhile, Vali killed Mayavi and escaped from the cave, arriving back in his kingdom to find Sugriva on the throne. In fury he denounced him, seized his wife and banished him.

'Since then I have lived in fear, wandering the forests and hills until I found shelter here in Rishyamukha, the only place where Vali cannot harm me. He can throw mountain peaks in the air and catch them and tear up large trees at will. But once he fought the demon Dundubhi, killing him by throwing him a distance of four miles. The demon's body landed near this place and splashed blood on the sage Matanga. He was so disturbed by this intrusion that he cursed Vali that if he or any of his monkeys ever set foot here they would be turned to stone. That is why we live here, because it is the only place where we are safe from him.

'Now that you know the strength of Vali, you will surely understand if I doubt whether you are strong enough to oppose him. No one has ever defeated him in combat, so how do I know you can do it? The skeleton of the demon Dundubhi lies nearby. If you can throw it with your foot a distance of one thousand yards, then you may be strong enough.'

Rama took up this challenge and, lifting the carcass with his toe, tossed it a hundred miles. But Sugriva was not satisfied.

'The carcass is dried up and lighter than when Vali threw it. I have another test for you. Sometimes Vali used to pierce these sal trees to practice his archery, splitting the trunk of a tree in two. If you can do that you are strong enough to defeat him.'

Close by were seven sal trees in a row. Rama took an arrow from his quiver and shot it from his bow. It passed through each of the trees in turn, then penetrated the earth as far as the underworld before bursting out again minutes later and re-entering his quiver. After seeing this feat, Sugriva bowed low in astonishment and was fully convinced of Rama's power to defeat Vali.

'Come then,' said Rama. 'Let us go to Kiskindha where you can challenge your brother to a duel.'

Rama and Lakshmana's alliance with Sugriva and Hanuman eventually leads them to fight side by side against the evil Ravana. Here they are shown together in the thick of battle.

THE DEATH OF VALI

Kiskindha, the capital of the Vanara kingdom, was built around a series of underground caves, with carved pillars and cascades of water. Here Vali lived in comfort with his wives. His peace was disturbed by the roaring of Sugriva, who stood outside challenging him to duel, with Rama concealed in the forest nearby.

The two brothers met with a thunderous clash, like Mercury crashing into Mars. Rama, concealed behind a tree, watched closely, his bow at the ready, waiting for an opportunity to strike Vali. But he was baffled. The brothers appeared identical and it was impossible for him to be sure which one was Vali.

Eventually Vali got the upper hand and Sugriva, battered and bleeding, was forced to retreat, running for his life to the safety of Rishyamukha. When Rama returned Sugriva was dismayed.

'You encouraged me to fight with Vali,' said Sugriva, 'saying you would kill him. But now I see it is as I feared: you don't have the strength to do it.'

'Let me explain,' replied Rama. 'I was unable to tell you and Vali apart and did not dare fire my arrow in case I killed you by accident. Next time you must wear some distinguishing mark.' So Lakshmana made a garland of flowering creepers and put it around Sugriva's neck, and they went back a second time.

At the entrance to Kiskindha, Sugriva let out a roar which split the air, frightening away all the forest animals. In response, Vali shook with rage and prepared to meet him. But his wife, Tara, was anxious.

'Quell your anger and don't let yourself be provoked. I feel uneasy about Sugriva coming a second time. I have heard that he has made friendship with Rama, son of the emperor of Ayodhya, who is invincible in battle. My advice is that you abandon this quarrel with your brother. Make him prince regent and give him gifts, and befriend Rama as well.' But Vali, in the grip of fate, did not heed Tara's advice.

'Why should I put up with his arrogance?' said Vali. 'And besides, Rama would never harm an innocent person such as me. I will fight again with Sugriva, so long as he stands up to me. He will soon run away again when he feels the blows of my fists.'

So Vali sallied forth, hissing like a snake. His brother Sugriva, shining golden-brown, tightened his cloth and waited for him. The two met once more, colliding like two bulls. Vali smashed Sugriva with his fist, making him vomit blood. Then Sugriva tore up a tree and struck Vali to the ground, making him shake. They locked in combat, each effulgent like the moon and sun in the sky. They fought with tree trunks, boulders, fists, feet, arms and legs, roaming about the forest smeared in blood like two storm clouds.

Vali started to get the upper hand and Sugriva desperately looked around for Rama. Seeing his chance, Rama let loose an arrow tipped with gold and silver. With a thunderous flash it tore into Vali's breast and knocked him to the ground. Uttering a cry of pain, he lay motionless. He was mortally wounded but he still had the strength to speak. He saw Rama with his bow and accused him.

'This is a cruel and dishonourable act, to kill someone who was not fighting against you. I never thought you would stoop to attack me in such a way. I did nothing against

HANUMAN

Hanuman carries the mountain of herbs which he brought from the Himalayas to save the lives of Rama and Lakshmana.

THE SON OF Vayu, the Wind god, Hanuman is popular for his good humour and selfless devotion to Rama. Worshipped at roadside shrines all over India, in *Ramayana* he is said to be superior in strength, wisdom, amiability and sweetness of temper.

Endowed with enormous strength and the gift of assuming any shape or form, his cunning, speed and agility make him an invaluable ally. Yet when Hanuman was young he misused his strength to play mischief, so that forest sages cursed him to be unaware of his power, making him meek and submissive. In *Ramayana*, Hanuman is granted a boon from Rama for his devotion. He chooses to live as long as men speak of Rama and his deeds, thereby securing him a place in contemporary Indian life.

you. I am an innocent monkey who lived in the forest eating only fruits and roots. Though you are born to be a king, you have no rights over me. You are a ruler of men, whereas I am a beast of the jungle who has done you no harm. What do you have to say in defence of your brutal behaviour?' Vali lapsed into silence, his mouth parched and his body racked with pain. Rama answered Vali with respect.

'Why do you reproach me? Listen to the reasons for my action. My brother Bharata is emperor of these lands and it is my duty, under his command, to uphold justice throughout his kingdom.

'You failed to give due protection to your younger brother, who you should treat as your own son, and moreover, you took his wife, Ruma. The punishment for one who has union with his brother's wife while his brother is alive is death.'

'These are my reasons for slaying you, as well as to fulfil my word to your brother that I would help him recover his wife and his kingdom. I have acted as law-keeper for your own good, because the religious laws state that a criminal justly punished is absolved of sin and ascends to heaven just as the pious do. Thus I have released you

from your sin and I have no regrets over what I have done.'

Vali sighed. 'What you have done is correct. I see that you are indeed devoted to the good of all people with a clear and unruffled mind. I beg you to fulfil my last request. Please see that my son Angada, who is still a boy, is reconciled with Sugriva and cared for by him, and see that Sugriva treats my widow, Tara, with kindness.'

'Do not worry on this score,' Rama reassured him.

'Forgive me,' whispered Vali.

Hearing news of her husband's condition, Tara hurried to him, crying and beating her head in agony. She came upon him lying on the ground like a spent cloud and clasped him to her bosom.

'Why don't you speak to me, my great hero? Why does my heart not break into a thousand pieces to see you in this state? You have got your reward for banishing your brother and stealing his wife. If only you had heeded my advice. Here is your son. Come darling Angada, see your father for the last time.'

Vali glimpsed his brother Sugriva standing before him.

'Forgive me, brother,' he murmured, 'I was carried away by forces out of my control. I am about to leave for the abode of death, and I want you to take the throne and rule over Kiskindha. Please look after my son Angada as if he were your own, and be considerate to Tara and always listen to her advice, for she speaks the truth.' Finally he spoke to his son. 'Accept Sugriva as your protector and serve him with devotion. Do not be over-fond of others nor without affection, but always seek the balance.' With these words Vali breathed his last.

Sugriva was overcome with remorse after hearing his brother's dying words and thought of ending his own life in recompense. Tara also wanted to die.

'You are wise and patient,' she prayed to Rama. 'Please kill me with the same arrow that killed my husband, then I can be reunited with him.'

'Do not despair,' Rama comforted them, 'for this world is made up of

Rama prepares to slay the monkey king Vali as he wrestles with his brother Sugriva.

happiness and sorrow in equal measure. Tara, you will yet find happiness under the protection of Sugriva, and your son will be prince regent, therefore do not lament.'

Rama then helped them with Vali's funeral. They carried his body in procession to a lonely spot by the river, where a funeral pyre was built and sacred hymns were chanted. As the hills echoed to the crying of his wives and the Vanara women, his body was enveloped in flames and he departed on his long journey to the next world. Rama patiently watched as Sugriva and his companions bathed in the river to purify themselves, then came towards him. Hanuman spoke up.

'We will now take Sugriva to Kiskindha and crown him. After he has been ceremonially anointed and bathed according to our customs, please come and feast with us in our capital.'

'Thank you, Hanuman,' replied Rama, 'but I cannot indulge in the comforts of Kiskindha. I must keep my vow to my father and stay in the forest until my fourteen years are up.'

Thus Sugriva, with the help of Rama, got back his wife Ruma and his kingdom and lived happily. Meanwhile, the monsoon season began and the rains made it impossible for Rama and his new allies to track down Ravana.

'You all enjoy yourselves,' said Rama. 'I will live with Lakshmana in this cave which is dry and airy with a nearby waterfall. In four months, when the rains are over, our search for Sita will begin.'

HINDU ASTROLOGY

THE HINDU system of astrology is very ancient; there are numerous references to it in the earliest Sanskrit texts, and in *Ramayana*.

It essentially differs from western astrology in that the signs of the zodiac are adjusted to take account of the procession of eqinoxes, and thus it is claimed to be more accurate. It also differs in that it links the influence of the planets to particular gemstones which are used to counteract negative influences. An integral part of Hindu astrology is an understanding of the transmigration of the soul and the effects of karma (see pp. 7, 52), which are responsible for the nature of a particular person's birthchart.

It is usual for Hindus to calculate a child's horoscope at the time of birth, and then refer to it when choosing a marriage partner and at other important times of life. In many walks of life, such as business and political affairs, astrology still plays a significant part in the lives of many Hindus.

GATHERING THE TRIBES

The rains intensified and Sugriva and Rama retired to their caves: Sugriva to the comfort of the cave-city of Kiskindha, and Rama to his hermit's cave in the forest.

The cave chosen by Rama and Lakshmana was ideal for their needs. It was near the wooded summit of Prasravana Hill, deep and dry and well sheltered from the rain-laden easterly winds. Close by was a rocky pool of lotus flowers and not far away a broad river with sandy banks.

Sitting at the entrance of the cave, Rama looked out through the rain. The earth steamed and dark clouds lashed the mountain sides. The flashes of lightning inside the dark clouds seemed to him like Sita struggling in the arms of Ravana, and the rain seemed like her tears.

The heat and dust of summer subsided and tracks became muddy and impassable. Mountain streams rushed to the sea, strewn with flowers and reddened by the earth, flocks of swans migrated to their northern homes and flights of herons flew beneath the clouds pealing with thunder.

Rama lay awake in the moonlit nights thinking of Sita. In the distance he could hear the beating drums and festive singing of the monkeys celebrating Sugriva's victory.

'Sugriva is enjoying his change of fortune,' he thought, 'while I have lost everything. But it is not yet time to act. We must wait for the rains to end, when Sugriva will remember his obligation to me.'

After four months Hanuman looked out and saw the sky clear and bright. The rains were over and the time had come to repay the debt to Rama. He went to Sugriva and found him intoxicated in the embrace of his wife Ruma.

'Do not forget your friend Rama who has done you good service by killing Vali,' reproved Hanuman. 'He is waiting to hear what you are doing to help him find Sita.' Sugriva was stirred into action.

'Call for Nila,' he commanded. 'Tell him to muster monkey troops from near and far. All monkey-warriors must be here within fifteen days under pain of death.' Sugriva then returned to the arms of his mistresses.

But Rama heard nothing. He felt the change of season as the warm autumn nights drew in under a clear sky. He called Lakshmana.

'Go and speak with Sugriva. Tell him not to forget that it was I who killed Vali, and warn him that if he does not help me I am quite capable of killing him too!'

Lakshmana set off in earnest to confront Sugriva. As he angrily entered the caves of Kiskindha the guards fled to inform Sugriva of his arrival. Sugriva, however, was in a drunken stupor in the midst of his lovers. Hanuman impressed upon him the seriousness of the situation.

'You have lost track of time. Now go quickly and appease Lakshmana,' he urged. 'Bow low before him and offer to do whatever Rama pleases.'

Lakshmana was ushered into Sugriva's private apartments. He saw beautiful girls decorated with tinkling ornaments. The lovely Tara, now Sugriva's wife, emerged in a languid state, slightly intoxicated with her girdle loosened.

'What displeases you, Prince Lakshmana?' she enquired softly.

'Your husband appears to have forgotten his duty,' replied Lakshmana. 'For the last four months he has indulged in wine and love-making and seems unaware that it is now time to fulfil his duty to Rama. I have come to remind him.'

'Please forgive my husband, who forgets the passing of time when under the sway of passion. However, he has already sent for thousands and millions of monkeys, and has quite shaken off his sensuous mood.' Tara beckoned him into Sugriva's presence, where he beheld Sugriva lying like a god on a soft couch embracing Ruma and served by young women, his eyes rolling with intoxication. Lakshmana angrily rebuked him.

'You are decadent and ungrateful. You have accepted Rama's services but have not returned them. Rama wishes me to warn you that if you do not honour your agreement with him you will go the way Vali went.' Sugriva got up quickly, scattering his women like the moon carrying stars in its wake.

'Do not speak harshly to my husband,' pleaded Tara, 'he meant no harm. To please

In their search for Sita, monkeys ransack desert caves and kill demons. In the background, Hanuman's party see birds emerging from a cave and decide to explore it.

Rama he would give up his throne and even Ruma and myself. He is prepared to kill Ravana, but we must first defeat Ravana's army, which is said to consist of a thousand billion rakshasas. Therefore we have sent for millions of monkeys, baboons and bears from the four quarters to assemble here. Today they are due to arrive.'

After Lakshmana had been placated by Tara's words, Sugriva ventured to speak.

'I owe my good fortune to Rama and I will repay him. Ask him to forgive me.'

'Forgive my harsh words, spoken out of concern for Rama,' countered Lakshmana. 'Now come with me to reassure him.'

'First I must organize the gathering of my troops.' Sugriva called again for his commander Nila. 'Send out a second wave of messengers to hasten the mustering of forces from the far-flung mountain ranges of Himalaya, Mahendra, Vindhya, Kailash and Mandara. All must gather here within ten days. Especially attend to those who are sensuous and lazy. Tell them they must obey my royal command or suffer death.' In a moment these messengers took to the air. Flying with the speed of mind along the migratory routes of the birds, they fanned out across the world to gather monkeys from seashores, mountains, forests and lakesides.

A vast horde of monkeys assembled – black monkeys from Anjana mountain, golden monkeys from the forests of the sunset, monkeys like lions from Kailash mountain, red monkeys from the Vidhya heights, others from the Himalaya range and the shores of the Milk Ocean. When all was in hand Lakshmana took Sugriva before Rama, to whom he bowed low.

'Now the time has come for our great adventure,' said Rama.

'At this very moment,' announced Sugriva, 'the leaders of monkeys, bears and baboons are on their way to join us from all over the world, followed by troops numbering thousands of millions.'

Rama embraced him. As they spoke a dust-cloud rose from all sides veiling the sun. The sky darkened and the earth vibrated with the rumble of millions of feet as innumerable monkeys poured into the valley from all sides,

Sugriva, leader of the monkeys, and Jambavan, lord of the bears, meet in counsel with Rama and Lakshmana.

led by their illustrious chiefs, each with the power to fight single-handedly with the gods. One by one the chiefs came forward to identify themselves to Sugriva and bow to Rama before being assigned a place for their troops.

'Now what would you have us do, lord?' asked Sugriva.

'First we must find out if Sita is still alive and where she is being held.' said Rama. 'Once we know that, we will decide upon our course of action.'

Sugriva called the chiefs together and divided them into four parties, each of which was assigned a different direction: east, south, west and north. They were told to search all the lands as far as the great mountains encircling the earth, beyond which no human or monkey is allowed to pass, and to return within one month. Whoever found Sita was promised ample reward. Among these chiefs, Hanuman was sent south with Angada, son of Vali, Nila, son of the Fire god, and Jambavan, lord of the bears and son of Brahma. Sugriva spoke with Hanuman.

'None is your equal, Hanuman. You have the speed and agility of your father, the Wind god. I am relying on you to find Sita.' Seeing Sugriva's confidence in Hanuman, Rama was convinced that he was the one who would find Sita, so he took him aside and spoke with him.

'Take this ring inscribed with my name and give it to Sita, so that she will know you to be my servant. Your courage and determination guarantee your success. I am depending on you.'

Hanuman took the ring, touched it to his head and then bowed at Lord Rama's feet. Shining like the moon in a clear sky, he set off with the sound of Rama's words ringing in his ears.

THE SEARCH FOR SITA

Once the teams of searchers had been dispatched, Sugriva returned to his life of leisure and Rama to waiting. A month passed and the searchers from the east, north and west returned empty-handed.

'We have explored the mountains, forests, rivers and seas. We have ransacked caves and dense thickets, and we have encountered and killed large demons, suspecting them to be Ravana. But we have found no sign of Sita. Our only hope now lies with Hanuman.'

Hanuman's party, however, was not to be seen. They had gone south, the direction in which it was known Sita had been carried, over the Vindhya mountains to the desert beyond, which was without water or food. With their strength and hope fading, they criss-crossed the region again and again, finding no trace of Sita.

When their month was nearly up, exhausted from hunger and thirst, they came to the mouth of a deep cave on the southern tip of the Indian peninsula. From inside the cave came a flow of cool, moist air and around its mouth grew dense green foliage.

*While monkeys fan out across the world in their search for Sita, Rama
entrusts Hanuman with his ring, to present to Sita as a token.*

Herons and swans emerged from the cave, their plumes wet and stained with the red
pollen of lotuses. They decided to venture inside the cave in search of water.

Holding hands, they penetrated the darkness. For a long time all was dark as they
journeyed ever deeper. Then they saw light ahead and heard the tinkling of running
water. They emerged into a cavern illuminated by a clear, soft light where they found
trees of gold, mansions of silver and gold, luscious fruits and heaps of gems. Gratefully
they satisfied their hunger and thirst and restored their strength and spirits. Then they
looked about them and saw the figure of a woman dressed in deer skin and bark,
shining with an aura of saintliness. Hanuman asked her who she was and to whom the
cave belonged.

'This cave was the home of the demon Maya, who embellished it by his mystic art,
but was slain by Indra. I am Svayamprabha, sent here to be its guardian.' Hanuman
told her of their search for Sita.

'Goddess, our strength is now restored by your generosity. How can we repay you?'

'I want nothing from you, but tell me how I can help you,' she replied.

'Show us out of this place. We must return to our king, Sugriva, by the appointed
time.' She instructed them to close their eyes and in an instant they were once more
in the bright sunlight outside the cave.

As their eyes grew accustomed to the daylight they saw that the season of spring
was already far advanced, the trees being heavy with blossom. Fear gripped them as

they realized that their allotted month was past. If they returned now, without any news of Sita, Sugriva would kill them.

In despair they decided to fast to death. Weeping, they sat down and prepared to die. However, a more immediate danger faced the monkeys. From far above unseen eyes saw them as a tasty meal sent by providence. Sampati, king of the vultures and older brother of Jatayu, was perched on the mountainside above the monkeys. He had not eaten for a long time, because he was crippled by the loss of his wings.

'I shall eat each of these monkeys one by one as they die of starvation,' he said. The monkeys heard this and looked up to see the huge vulture.

'Jatayu, lord of vultures, gave his life for Rama,' protested Angada. 'Must we, who have sacrificed so much in the service of Rama, be eaten by this vulture?' Sampati was bewildered to hear mention of his brother Jatayu, and the name of Rama, who he knew to be the glorious son of Emperor Dasaratha.

'Who is it that speaks of Jatayu, my brother, and of Rama, son of Dasaratha? Help me down from my perch so that I may speak with you.'

The monkeys, who were past caring, thought they may as well die as food for this venerable vulture as by starvation, so they helped him down. They told Sampati the full story of Sita's abduction, Jatayu's death and the monkey's failure to find Sita and their consequent state of despair. Sampati was distressed to hear of the death of his younger brother Jatayu, and eager to help in the search for Sita.

'I will not eat you,' he said. 'Instead I can help you find Sita. I once saw from this mountain a beautiful young woman carried through the air by Ravana, calling the names "Rama! Lakshmana!"'

'This was surely Sita,' exclaimed Hanuman. 'Where did Ravana take her?'

'Ravana lives in the city of Lanka on an island a thousand miles out to sea. Sita is held captive there by Ravana.'

On hearing Sampati's information the monkeys leapt to their feet, all thoughts of starvation banished from their minds. Excitedly they took leave of Sampati and made their way to the nearby shore of the Indian Ocean. Looking across the southern sea they saw only the vast expanse of water and their hearts began to sink. How could they cross such a

In this Bengali devotional painting of Hanuman,
he is shown opening his heart to reveal his
beloved Sita and Rama.

great distance as a thousand miles? Each of them estimated his ability in leaping: some said they could leap one hundred miles, some two, some five hundred, but none felt confident enough to cross to Lanka and back. Jambavan turned to Hanuman, who had kept silent.

'You are son of the Wind god and are equal to him in your power to fly through the air. When you were a child you saw the sun rising through the trees and mistook it for a fruit. You leapt into the sky to catch it, rising to a height of twenty thousand miles. In anger at your audacity, Indra hurled his thunderbolt at you and dashed you to the ground, breaking your jaw. Therefore you are called Hanuman, meaning 'one with a broken jaw'. To make up for this Indra blessed you to meet death only when you choose to die, and Brahma made you invulnerable in combat. Now show us your prowess by leaping across the vast ocean to Lanka.'

While Jambavan spoke Hanuman shook off his depression and grew to a colossal size. Whirling his tail in delight, he prepared to leap across the ocean.

'I can overtake the sun on its journey from east to west, or jump to the very ends of the earth, scattering clouds and shaking mountains. Certainly I will jump to Lanka.'

Looking for a secure foothold from which to leap, giant Hanuman climbed the nearby Mount Mahendra. As he trod on it the mountain trembled, releasing new springs and alarming deer and elephants, driving snakes from their holes. Concentrating his mind, Hanuman fixed his thoughts on Lanka and the divine Sita, and prepared to jump.

THE FOUR VARNAS

TRADITIONAL Hindu society is divided into four varnas, or social groups, which are compared to different parts of the body. The brahmanas, or priests and teachers, are the head of the social body, supplying intelligence and direction; the kshatriyas, or ruling class, are the arms, supplying administration and protection; the vaishyas, or farmers and business people, are the stomach, giving prosperity; and the sudras, or workers, are the legs providing skills and labour. Originally, membership of a varna was supposed to be based on personal merit, but a rigid caste system developed, with a proliferation of sub-castes into which people were forced by birth, while those without caste, such as the tribal 'outcasts', were often denied basic rights. Today social reforms have relaxed or abolished the strict caste system, although it still dominates rural areas and dictates marriage partners.

However, the basic system of varnas has given Hindu society great stability and continuity over thousands of years.

THE FIFTH BOOK

Sundara Kanda

*Reaching the island of Lanka, Hanuman shrinks to
the size of a cat and searches the golden city of Lanka.
He eventually discovers Sita imprisoned in the ashok
grove beside Ravana's palace, guarded by demon
women. Here, Hanuman hides in a tree-top, watching
as Ravana begs Sita to be his queen. Ravana is
accompanied by girls carrying torches and is
restrained by his wife, Mandodari.*

THE KINGDOM OF LANKA

ACROSS THE OCEAN

ANUMAN CROUCHED LOW on the slopes of Mount Mahendra, stretching out his tail and fixing his eyes on the horizon. He remembered his father the Wind god and prayed for his protection. Then he vowed, 'Either I shall find Sita or destroy Lanka,' and leaped into the sky.

As he launched himself the mountain shook, sending forth showers of fragrant flowers. Thousands of trees were uprooted and swept into the sky, falling like a carpet of stars into the sea. He flew through the air with his tail out behind him, shining like the sun as he passed in and out of clouds. His eyes blazed and the wind thundered past his ears while far below the sea tossed in his wake, churning up waves as high as mountains.

Wishing to help Hanuman, the Sea god sent the winged mountain Mainaka up from the seabed to give him a resting place. But as the mountain, with its gold-tipped peaks, rose before him, Hanuman simply thrust it aside with his chest. The gods were thrilled at his prowess and wanted to see more of his splendour, so they sent Surasa, mother of the Naga celestial snakes, to test him. She assumed a gigantic form and rose from the ocean in front of Hanuman, with her mouth outstretched to devour him. But Hanuman expanded his size, forcing her to open her mouth wider, then shrank to the size of a thumb to enter and leave her mouth in an instant, and continued on his way.

Next came the sea-demoness Simhika, who had not eaten for years. When she saw Hanuman flying above the sea, she used her magic powers to seize his shadow. Hanuman felt himself held back by some unseen influence and looked down, seeing Simhika in the sea. He swept down towards her and she tried to swallow him, but he again shrank to nothing and flew into her mouth. Penetrating deep inside her, he burst out through her heart and killed her instantly.

As he neared the island of Lanka, Hanuman saw forests and mountains stretched out below him, and in the distance Mount Trikuta, beside which stood the fabulous city of Lanka, looking like the capital of heaven. He returned to his normal size and touched down safely on the peak of Mount Trikuta. Not even short of breath, he set off through the lush jungle towards the city. Soon he arrived at the edge of the outer moat beneath towering walls and turrets of gold with pennants fluttering in the breeze. He made his way to the northern gate where he saw large numbers of guards and much coming and going. He lay hidden among the trees until darkness fell.

When all was dark he shrank to the size of a cat and sprang over the battlements. By the light of the full moon he followed the main highway into the city. Around him were mansions of gold inlaid with diamonds and pearls. Deep rumblings, like the distant roar of the ocean, came from the depths of the city, and here and there bells tinkled. Suddenly he was challenged by a hideous female figure.

'Who are you and what do you want?' she demanded.

'First tell me who you are,' Hanuman replied.

'My name is Lanka, the guardian spirit of this city, and I am aware of all that goes on here. No one can wander about this city without my sanction.'

'It is my wish to see around Lanka and I shall do as I please,' retorted Hanuman.

'Not without overcoming me,' she cried, and struck Hanuman on the face. In retaliation he felled her to the ground with a slap.

HINDU PAINTING

THE OLDEST surviving paintings in India are on the walls of the Ajanta caves in the south, some dating from the second century BC. Mural painting, with bold designs and vivid colours, continued to develop in the region, portraying vast scenes from the religious epics in caves, temples and palaces.

The traditional palm-leaf manuscripts used for religious texts in India were often illuminated with miniature paintings. Under the influence of Persian manuscript painting, these evolved in the north of the country to produce the Rajasthan schools of miniature painting, beginning from the fifteenth century.

These schools were patronized by Mughal rulers and Hindu maharajas and developed many styles, such as Kangra and Basohli, with an emphasis on delicately-coloured landscapes and fine drawing. They have been used to illustrate this book, along with examples of folk art from Bengal and images from the murals of the south.

'Spare me,' she begged. 'I was once told by Brahma that when a monkey enters Lanka and overpowers me, the defeat of all the rakshasas who live here will soon follow. I give you permission to go wherever you please and assure you that you will accomplish your purpose, and in so doing bring about the destruction of Ravana.'

Hanuman continued on his way. Soon he heard laughter and music and saw on the streets people of all kinds. Some were ugly, others beautiful, some coarse, others refined. He saw scholars and priests, powerful warriors and drunken fools. Naked ascetics with shaven heads muttered malevolent spells and eyed him curiously as he

Hanuman leaps across the rooftops of the city of Lanka, looking for Sita; he searches Ravana's private palace where he sees Ravana's wives, but not the princess.

passed, while monstrous demons with deformed features and misshapen bodies guarded doorways along the way, armed with swords, clubs and spears.

After passing many mansions and crossing wide avenues, Hanuman came to the outer gates of Ravana's palace, made of solid gold embellished with precious gems. Inside was a city within a city, filled with mansions of gold and silver, teeming with demons strutting here and there, challenging each other in proud tones, singing boisterously or lying in drunken stupor. He also saw noble beings, handsome and graceful, dressed in finery and shining brightly.

Entering the inner palace, Hanuman passed armed guards mounted on chariots and throngs of courtiers in avenues vibrant with the sound of kettledrums and trumpets. He came upon rakshasa women, some bashful, some alluring – all exceptionally beautiful. He looked at them all closely, hoping to find Sita, but saw her nowhere.

He ranged among the houses of Ravana's generals and ministers, and his brothers Kumbhakarna and Vibhisana. He passed Ravana's stables, which housed mighty war elephants and horses of many colours, and then he entered gardens and pleasure grounds resounding with the cries of peacocks and sparkling with heaps of gems.

Finally he reached Ravana's personal residence. Blazing with jewels, it was a palace of such splendour it seemed as if heaven had come down to earth. In its inner courtyard was moored the fabulous Puspaka airplane, like a mountain, with domes clustered one above another. This was the airplane that Ravana had stolen from Kuvera, the treasurer of the gods, and was his proudest possession. It was built from gold, silver, coral and crystal; yet it hovered weightless above the ground. Hanuman slipped aboard, up stairways of gems, through pillared halls laid with crystal and lit by emeralds and sapphires. Fountains played in lotus pools surrounded by groves of artificial trees and flowers. The Puspaka was capable of travelling at the speed of mind along cosmic pathways. It was imbued with a mind of its own, which responded to the thoughts of its commander, who must have exceptional power in order to control it. Hanuman scoured all the chambers and hallways on its many levels, but did not find Sita.

From there he stole into Ravana's private apartments where he saw bevies of gorgeous women deep in slumber, exhausted from their revelries, their limbs and coverings in disarray. With their heads pillowed on one another's breasts and arms, their garlands and necklaces scattered, and their breath perfumed by fragrant wines, they looked like swans floating on a sea of lotus flowers. Lamps burned dimly, held by sentinels of gold who watched silently over the fair assembly.

In the midst of this scene was a raised bedstead of ivory and gold beneath a white canopy where Ravana slept, fanned by female attendants. His powerful arms, encircled with gold bracelets and flashing with diamonds, revealed the scars of many battles. Around his bed slept female musicians, still holding their musical instruments in sensuous embrace.

On a richly upholstered bed nearby lay a fair-complexioned woman more gorgeous than the others. At first Hanuman thought her to be Sita, but then he realized this could not be so; Sita would never surrender herself to be enjoyed by Ravana. This woman must be Ravana's queen, Mandodari, who had been given to him as a young girl by her father, the demon Maya. Since then Ravana had carried off thousands of other young girls from the homes of gods and celestial beings, all of whom were allured by his power and sexual energy. Sita, however, was the one woman who would never submit to his will.

Continuing his search, Hanuman entered the dining hall, where meats such as peacock, rhinoceros and porcupine stood untouched or half-consumed on golden dishes. The floor was scattered with broken cups and bowls amid piles of disordered cushions, pools of juice and half-finished cups of wine.

Leaving the palaces, Hanuman scoured the open spaces surrounding them. He looked among the crowds at crossroads, in narrow lanes, in chasms and ravines, but not seeing Sita anywhere, he began to fear the worst. Perhaps she had fallen into the sea as she was carried to Lanka, or been set upon by the demon women in Ravana's employ, or had died from a broken heart in separation from her lord. In despondency Hanuman decided to hide somewhere and fast to death, his mission having failed.

Just then he came across a grove of ancient ashok trees that he had not noticed before, hidden beneath a wooded hilltop beside Ravana's palace. This was Ravana's private retreat and something told Hanuman it might be the place where he would find Sita. He prayed to Vishnu to give him success, and leaped over the boundary wall. Inside, the trees were thick with flowers and entwined with climbers. As the monkey jumped from one tree to another they scattered their blossoms, covering him with petals so that he looked like the spirit of spring. Advancing deeper into the grove he found that the trees took on a silver hue, and their flowers became richer and more perfumed. Water tumbled down the hillside into a crystal-clear pool with a white sandy bed sparkling with gems and corals. Around the pool, marble steps descended from among trees of gold that chimed as if with tiny bells in the breeze. Hanuman climbed the tallest tree and peered out from its branches across the moonlit landscape. Nearby was a tree greater and more venerable that all the others. Beneath it he saw a woman seated on the ground dressed in torn unwashed clothes. She was pale and drawn and her face was bathed in tears, but her beauty shone like the moon through a veil of clouds.

Hanuman knew her to be the same woman he had seen carried over Rishyamukha Hill by Ravana, and he recognized the ornaments she wore as matching the ones cast down from the sky to the monkeys that day, and her yellow robe as matching the silk cloth in which they had been wrapped. She must be Sita.

Around her demonesses circled restlessly, hideous in appearance, carrying clubs or spikes. Some had only one eye and misshapen features, some were covered in hair, some were hump-backed or monstrous in size, with heads of goats, camel's feet or donkey's ears. In the midst of these monsters, Sita was weighed down by grief, like a boat sinking beneath its load.

'How can such a blameless and exalted soul as Sita be afflicted with so much sorrow?' lamented Hanuman. 'Indeed it is hard to understand destiny. Yet I see she is forbearing as the earth from whom she was born. She does not see the monsters surrounding her, or this heavenly garden. She sees only Rama.'

THE RING

As dawn approached Hanuman heard the distant sound of the sacred hymns of the Vedas being chanted in the city. At Ravana's bedside musicians serenaded him and slowly the great demon stirred, his head heavy with drink. His first thought was of Sita. Although he was powerful beyond measure, Ravana was the slave of passion, and at the moment all his passion was focused on Sita. Dressing and perfuming himself, he set off to the ashok grove followed by a procession of female attendants bearing torches in the early dawn light. As it passed through the glades echoing with birdsong, the procession looked like the progress of the god of love.

Hidden among the branches, Hanuman watched as Ravana approached. As soon as she saw him, Sita huddled up in modesty and shook with fear. Although she was distressed and forlorn, she could not hide her flawless beauty, which shone like the moon through the clouds. Hanuman was amazed to see the mighty Ravana actually prostrate himself full-length on the ground before her.

'Have no fear, sweet lady, no other demons lurk here. It is only I, begging for your love,' came Ravana's love-stricken words. 'My soul is ravished by you. Please return my love. It is the habit of us demons to seduce other's wives by force, but I have

restrained from this for ten months, waiting for you to willingly give yourself to me.

'Your beauty holds me entranced. The creator, after fashioning you, must have retired, having surpassed all else. Though you are covered in torn cloth with your hair in a single plait, you make me forget even my consort Mandodari. My thousands of other wives will wait upon you. Why do you think only of Rama, a mere man? He is nothing compared to me. Untold wealth can be yours. Just be mine.'

'Take your mind off me and be satisfied with your many wives,' Sita responded fiercely. 'You should protect me, not seek to molest me. Your infatuation will destroy your kingdom and all who live in it. I belong to Rama as the sunshine belongs to the sun. You will never have me. Soon Rama will be here with arrows of fire to destroy you. You cannot flee – he will find you wherever you are.'

'It seems, good lady, that the more I speak sweet words to you the more unkind you become. Very well, be warned; you have two months to surrender to me. If you refuse to share my bed after that time, you will be minced up and I will eat you for my breakfast!'

These foul words upset many of Ravana's women, whom he had won from among gods or pious families. They tried to reassure Sita with secret glances. But she continued fearlessly.

'You have no friends here, otherwise they would advise you that you bring upon yourself your own destruction by stealing another's wife, not to speak of the wife of Rama. I wonder that your tongue has not fallen out, or your eyes been blinded. I am here for your destruction. Touch me at your peril.'

Ravana's face twisted and he raised his hand to strike Sita, but was restrained by his women, who dragged him away.

'Sport with us, lord, and have nothing more to do with this Sita,' they implored.

'Do with her as you will to force her to her senses,' he shouted at those around Sita. Angry and humiliated, he left. Now the demonesses came forward, first cajoling, then taunting, threatening Sita with their weapons.

'Don't you know what you are turning down? You have been loyal to your husband, now do the sensible thing. Ravana has vanquished the entire universe. The thirty-three high gods and even Indra himself are under his sway, and now he wishes to give up his wife Mandodari in favour of you. You are mad to refuse.'

'I would like to taste her liver,' snarled one, 'and her heart, too.'

'Why should we wait?' cried another. 'Divide her up now and cook her.'

'I will never be his wife,' Sita retorted. 'I am human, and he is a rakshasa and I will never have anything to do with the monster. You can eat me if you like, I don't care.'

Shuddering with emotion she withdrew towards the tree in which Hanuman was concealed. 'I would not touch that despicable Ravana even with my left foot. Why can I not die now? Then I would be shamed no more.

'If Rama would come, he would kill Ravana and destroy this entire city. Then it will

Sita is held captive and tormented by ugly rakshasa women, while Hanuman, hidden in the tree, gives her Rama's ring as token of Rama's love and proof that he is Rama's messenger.

be you who weep, your husbands dead. He will destroy you all.' An old rakshasa woman, named Trijata, awoke just then. Seeing that the other rakshasas were tormenting Sita, she stopped them.

'Eat one another if you like, but you will never eat her. I have had a dream,' she murmured, 'I saw Rama, dressed in shining white, riding with Sita on a great white elephant. Then I saw Ravana and his brothers, their heads shaven, riding south on mules, laughing hideously. Next I saw a powerful monkey set fire to the city of Lanka which fell crashing into the waves, while the women of the city laughed in madness. My advice to you is stay away from her and leave this place if you can.'

Her companions fell silent and sat down listlessly, not caring enough to argue. Sita crept further into the hollow of the tree beneath Hanuman. Fingering the cord tying her hair, she thought of suicide.

Hanuman desperately wanted to reassure Sita. But how could he do so without frightening her? She would think he was just another of Ravana's tricks. He decided to talk in Sanskrit, the human language spoken in Ayodhya. Softly, he spoke of Rama.

'There was once a mighty emperor in the line of Iksvaku called Dasaratha, who had a son named Rama,' he began, and went on to recite the tale of Rama's exploits up to the time that Sita was carried away.

'In search of Sita, Rama and Lakshmana journeyed south where they met with Sugriva, lord of the monkeys. In alliance with him a great search for Sita was begun, bringing me to Lanka where I have at last found her. Even now, Rama is waiting for me to bring back news so that he can rescue her.'

In rapture, Sita listened to this mysterious voice, thinking at first it was just a dream. She looked here and there until she caught sight of Hanuman in the tree above her. Was this an apparition? How could a monkey talk, and know all these details of her history?

Sita, while she shelters under the tree, hears Hanuman's voice, and demands proof from him that he is a genuine messenger of Rama.

'I hope this monkey's words are true,' she whispered to herself. Encouraged, Hanuman slipped from the tree, staying hidden from the rakshasas.

'Gentle lady with lotus eyes, who are you and why do you cry? Are you truly Sita the wife of Rama, or a goddess fallen from heaven?'

'I am Sita, daughter of Janaka. I lived in Ayodhya with my husband Rama for twelve years before following him to the forest in exile. There we lived in peace served by his brother Lakshmana, until the evil Ravana, who now torments me, carried me away. If my husband does not come to rescue me I have two months to live.'

'Dear lady, Rama wishes you to know that he and Lakshmana are both well. He also wants to know of your welfare.' Hanuman came nearer to Sita, but she retreated in fear.

'If you are Ravana come to give me more pain, then stop! It is not right that you torture me so,' she tremored. 'But if you are who you say you are – and I pray it to be so – then please tell me about my dear Rama.'

'The glorious Rama brings happiness to the whole universe,' spoke Hanuman. 'He gives protection to all and punishes the wicked. Before long he will come here with a great army of monkeys to rescue you and kill Ravana.'

'How did you meet with Rama and how on earth did an alliance between humans and monkeys come about?' Sita demanded to know. 'Prove to me that you know Rama by describing him.'

Hanuman described in detail the appearance of Rama. He went on to explain how Rama had made friends with Sugriva and helped him defeat his brother Vali, and how Sugriva had gathered the monkey forces to help Rama find Sita, concluding with the story of his own search, his meeting with Sampati and his decision to leap over the sea to Lanka.

'I am Hanuman, son of the Wind god and minister of Sugriva. Doubt me no more.'

Reassured by all she heard, Sita trembled with relief. Tears of happiness fell from her long eyelashes and her face shone like the moon. Hanuman then produced Rama's ring and handed it to Sita, who recognized it as the one worn by her husband. Gazing on it as if it were Rama himself, she thanked Hanuman.

'You are a brave and powerful monkey to come all this way for me, crossing the ocean so wide and taking such risks. I owe you a debt of gratitude. But tell me, why has Rama not yet come to rescue me? Has he given up hope or stopped loving me?'

'He does not know where you are. As soon as I get back he will lead a powerful army to rescue you. Rama thinks only of you; he lies awake at night with tears in his eyes, and in his sleep he calls your name.'

Sita was both glad and pained to hear of Rama's grief. She begged Hanuman to act fast, for she could not survive much longer.

'Let me rescue you this moment,' exclaimed Hanuman. 'Climb on my back and I will take you to the presence of Rama this very day.'

'Now you are talking just like a monkey,' laughed Sita. 'How could I go anywhere on your back?' Hanuman had forgotten that he was only the size of a cat. He began to grow until he towered above her. With blazing eyes and swishing tail he proudly declared that if he wished he could carry away the whole of Lanka.

'Now I see your full power,' agreed Sita, 'and I do not doubt you could carry me through the air. But I might fall or lose my life travelling so fast and so high in the sky, and it is not right for me willingly to touch any other male than my husband. Let Rama come here and defeat Ravana, then take me back to Ayodhya himself. That will be most fitting.'

'If you cannot come with me, please give me some token to take to Rama,' requested Hanuman. Sita unwrapped a large jewel from her cloth.

'Give him this,' she said. 'He will recognize it. And ask him if he remembers the time when he decorated my cheek with mineral dye after the rains.' Holding the precious jewel tightly, Hanuman prepared to leave.

'Tell him to come soon. I will not be able to survive here for more than a month.'

'Have no fear, lady, Rama will soon be here,' he said, and was gone.

A CHALLENGE TO RAVANA

Hanuman did not go far. Reaching the edge of the grove, he paused to consider his position. He had found Sita. Now he decided to try the strength of the rakshasa forces and deal out some punishment. He also wanted to get a closer look at Ravana. So he decided to provoke some attention.

Returning to the grove, he started uprooting trees. Soon the whole grove lay devastated, save the great tree under which Sita sheltered. Satisfied, Hanuman sat on the arch over the gateway and waited.

Before long, eighty thousand troops arrived, armed with mallets and clubs. They surrounded Hanuman and attacked him. Armed with an iron bar and roaring loudly he leaped upon them, killing large numbers. Only a few managed to escape. Hearing of this defeat, Ravana sent the powerful warrior Jambumali, who arrived in a chariot drawn by donkeys. He had a ferocious appearance, but unfortunately he was no match for Hanuman, and soon lay dead. Hanuman once more sat upon the gateway, filled with the excitement of battle. Ravana now became exceedingly angry and sent the sons of his chief minister to deal with this impetuous monkey. Bringing with them a large army, these mighty warriors were ambitious to show off their strength. They showered Hanuman with arrows. He flew up into the sky, dodging the arrows, then dived upon them, beating them with his bare fists and tearing them with his nails. Soon they too lay dead on the battlefield. When Ravana heard this news he tried to conceal his dismay, and sent forth five of his most powerful generals, warning them to remain alert at all times.

'The creature may be produced by Indra for our demise. I have heard of strong monkeys, like Vali and Sugriva, but none like this. Capture him for interrogation.'

The generals went forth, but they fared no better, although in order to defeat them

Hanuman had to grow a great deal in size. Now he sat on the gateway like an angel of death.

Ravana next turned to his son Aksa, who though young was truly a great fighter. When Hanuman saw him, armoured in gold and mounted on a chariot that shone like the sun, he was surprised at his youth, and felt honoured to recognize him as a son of Ravana. The boy rushed at him with fury, pleasing Hanuman with his courage. Hanuman took to the air but the boy followed, flying in the sky in his chariot. Hanuman was sorry to have to kill this youth, but feared that if he did not he would prove a serious danger in the future. He smashed his chariot, but the boy flew in the sky by his own power, attacking Hanuman with his sword. At this Hanuman caught hold of his legs and wheeled him around in the air so fast that the boy passed out, then hurled him to the ground with tremendous force, breaking his limbs and killing him.

Ravana was afraid and grieved at the death of his son. He called his eldest son, Indrajit, his greatest fighter. Indrajit was so named because he had conquered Indra, the king of heaven, in single combat. He had been given special weapons and powers by Brahma and was the most feared demon warrior in the universe.

'Do not try to kill him,' advised Ravana, 'he seems invincible. Use the weapon given to you by Brahma to capture him and bring him to me.'

Indrajit went forth on a chariot drawn by four tigers. Hanuman recognized his

*Sita, a prisoner in the ashok grove, gives Hanuman a large jewel
to take back to Rama as proof that she is alive.*

HINDU FESTIVALS

RELIGIOUS festivals, of which only a few can be mentioned here, form a vital part in the life of every Hindu. They follow the Hindu calendar, which is based on lunar months.

In the month of Chaitra (March to April) which marks the beginning of the year, Ramanavami honours the birth of Rama. Much celebration occurs in the Vaishnava temples, particularly in the state of Uttar Pradesh at Ayodhya, the birthplace of Rama.

In the month of Ashadha (June to July), the spectacular Rathayatra festival occurs at Puri, on India's east coast, to celebrate Jagannath, 'Lord of the universe', who is a form of Krishna. Images of Jagannath, his brother Baladeva and his sister Subhadra are pulled on temple-chariots through the streets by a crowd of millions.

During the Rahki Bandham festival in the north and west of the country on the full moon of Shravan, young girls tie bracelets of silk and cord on their brother's wrists as a token of their loyalty to each other.

The month of Bhadra (August to September) sees the festival of Janmastami. On this day, temples stay open until midnight, the hour of Krishna's birth, and an image of Krishna is publicly bathed.

The birth of Ganesha, the elephant god, is also celebrated in this month.

In Mumbai (Bombay), the custom is to carry an image of Ganesha in procession and throw it into the sea.

In Navaratri (October), nine days of dancing and festivities are held in honour of the Mother Goddess Durga, the consort of Shiva.

The festival of Divali, in the month of Kartik (October to November), marks the Hindu New Year and is a time for closing business accounts, but is perhaps better known as the time when lamps and candles are lit in the streets and houses to welcome Rama and Sita home to Ayodhya.

Celebrated at the full moon of Phalgun (February to March), Holi is a spring festival commemorating the play of Krishna, when he and his friends sprayed coloured dyes on one another. It is an occasion for carnival and wild play. Holi also celebrates the rescue of the devotee Prahlada from fire by the demoness Holika, and is marked by bonfires in the streets.

Many festivals celebrate the story of *Ramayana*, such as Ramanavami, Divali and Sita's birthday in Vaisakha (April to May). The feast of the monkey god Hanuman occurs on the full moon of Chaitra, known as the festival of Hanuman Jayanti. For the Dusshera festival in October, giant effigies of Ravana the demon king are erected and burnt amid fireworks and pageantry.

assailant and thrilled at the prospect of fighting him. The two met head to head and an immense duel ensued. Wherever Hanuman flew Indrajit followed, but could not reach him with his arrows. Finally he saw his moment and released his Brahma weapon, which bound its victim with unbreakable bonds. Hanuman suddenly found himself unable to move, caught in Indrajit's snare. He plummeted to the ground and lost consciousness. Coming to, he realized that he had been overcome by a weapon belonging to Brahma, from whom he had special protection. He knew that he had nothing to fear from such a weapon and that he could get free from it if he wanted to, but he decided to let it bind him. He wanted to be brought before Ravana.

'Who is this creature?' demanded Ravana, 'and who has sent him? Roast him alive and we will eat him.'

Hanuman, bound with ropes, stood before Ravana, who was seated on a throne of crystal inlaid with jewels. His many eyes glowed copper-coloured, his sharp teeth gleamed, a mass of jewels covered his chest and his twenty arms were encircled by heavy gold bangles. Dazzled by his magnificence, Hanuman thought that if it were not for his antagonism to Rama, he might have protected the universe and been loved by all. Instead, because of his cruelty, he was universally feared and hated.

'Do not be afraid, monkey,' said Ravana's chief minister. 'Just tell us who sent you and you will come to no harm.'

'I am Hanuman, messenger of Rama,' answered Hanuman, 'who lost his wife Sita in Dandaka Forest. My master, Sugriva, made an alliance with Rama and offered to help him find her. I was deputed to look for her and my search brought me here to Lanka, where I have now found her.'

Turning to Ravana he spoke boldly. 'If you know what is good for you, you will release this woman. It is most sinful to steal another's wife. If you insist on holding her, you will bring destruction upon yourself and your kingdom. No one in this universe can withstand the anger of Rama. You think you are protected by the benediction you received from Brahma, but Rama is a human and Sugriva a monkey. From them you have no protection.

'I can destroy Lanka on my own, but it is Rama's wish to perform this task himself. Rama can create and destroy unlimited worlds and all the beings in them. He personally wishes to punish the demon who dares lay hands on his wife Sita. No one in this universe can withstand him, for he is the equal of Vishnu himself.'

Ravana, beside himself with rage at Hanuman's speech, ordered his death. But his brother Vibhisana intervened.

'My lord, do not give way to anger. This monkey is a messenger, and messengers may be punished, but not killed. Furthermore, you need him to carry back your challenge to his masters. To assert your supremacy, you must gather your army and punish Rama for daring to oppose you.'

This was acceptable to Ravana, who relented in favour of a better idea.

Captured as Rama's spy, Hanuman is brought before Ravana. As a punishment,
Hanuman's tail is wrapped, oiled then set alight before he is paraded in
shame through the streets of Lanka.

LANKA IN FLAMES

'Set light to his tail! That will be a suitable punishment for this spy,' taunted Ravana.
'Take him through the market places and humiliate him, then release him to return
wretched and mutilated to his kinsmen.'

Hanuman's tail was wrapped in cotton and soaked in oil, then set alight. Although
it was painful, Hanuman did not wince. He welcomed the opportunity to be taken a
second time around Lanka, this time during daylight, when he could see more
clearly. Allowing himself to be dragged around, he became a spectacle to women
and children. Meanwhile he carefully memorized the layout of the city and the
strength of its fortifications.

News was brought to Sita of his humiliation, and she prayed to the fire god for his
protection: 'If ever I have earned any credit by my penances, let Hanuman feel you as
cool.' From the moment of Sita's prayer Hanuman felt no discomfort from the flames.

'How is it that these flames feel cool like ice?' he thought. 'It must be the blessing
of Sita.' Feeling encouraged, Hanuman freed himself from his bonds and seized hold
of an iron club. In no time he dispatched his guards, swishing his tail in a circle of fire.

'I have laid waste to the grove and killed a good many rakshasas,' he thought, 'now I will set alight this whole city with the fire burning on my tail.' He leapt across the roofs of the houses, setting light to one after another. He worked his way towards the mansions of Ravana's generals and ministers, setting them all alight until even Ravana's palace was ablaze, yet he was careful to avoid the house of Vibhisana, who had saved his life. As he went he shouted, 'Victory to Rama.'

The wind blew and spread the blaze, transforming it into a fire-storm so intense that molten gold mixed with gems and pearls poured out of the collapsing buildings. The people of Lanka ran screaming through the streets as the whole city went up in flames. A great sheet of flame enveloped the hilltop and dense columns of black smoke ascended into the sky. The fire consumed rakshasas, horses, chariots and elephants – all that lived in the city, though the flames would not burn Hanuman.

Satisfied with his work, he left the city and quenched his tail in the sea. It was only then that the terrible thought occurred to him: what about Sita? He rushed back and found her safe, for she too had been protected by the Fire god.

'Dear son, you have done well,' she said. 'I wish you would stay and rest here for the night, for so long as you are here you bring me comfort. But it is better that you go at once and bring Rama, so that he can himself defeat Ravana and rescue me. Only my fear is that he will not be able to cross the ocean with all the monkeys.'

'Sugriva with his monkey warriors, and Rama and Lakshmana will soon be here. Do not doubt it, you will see him very soon.'

He climbed to the top of Mount Arista and once more leaped over the ocean. He flew through the clouds as before, and as he reached the other side let out a great roar of triumph. On the opposite shore, Hanuman's companions waited patiently for his return. They heard his victorious cry, and knew that he must have been successful. As he landed they rushed to meet him, gathering around him with hands folded in greeting and offerings of roots and fruits. Hanuman cried, 'Sita is found!' and they all sat down in a comfortable place to hear his story.

'No one is equal to you in courage or strength. Thanks to you we can be sure of receiving Rama's grace,' pronounced Angada. 'Now tell us everything so that we can decide what to do next.' Hanuman told them all that had happened, leaving out no details save Sita's personal messages for Rama. In excitement the monkeys proclaimed they should all go to Lanka to kill Ravana and rescue Sita. All were in favour, but Jambavan, the aged bear, wisely intervened.

'My friends, we were instructed to find Sita, nothing more. I don't doubt our capacity to finish the job, but Rama has vowed to win back Sita himself. We must leave that honour to him.'

All agreed with Jambavan's advice, so they set off at once

for Kiskindha to give the news to Rama, leaping through the air with Hanuman at their head. Near to Kiskindha was a garden called Madhuvana, famous for its wild honey. They decided to rest there and replenish their strength after having fasted for so long in the wilderness. They also felt they deserved a celebration.

Monkeys love to get intoxicated on wild honey, and soon they had consumed all the honeycombs. They celebrated with abandon, breaking trees, wrestling, laughing and crying, and trampling all over the beautiful garden of Madhuvana. An elderly monkey called Dadhimukha, appointed by Sugriva to look after the garden, did his best to ward them off, but he and his assistants was severely beaten. He ran to Sugriva to complain. When Sugriva heard that Hanuman and his party were misbehaving he understood the situation very well.

'Do you know what this means?' he laughed. 'It means they have found Sita! Tell them they are forgiven and that I want to see them immediately.'

By the time Dadhimukha got back, he found the monkeys in a more sober state. He apologized to them and passed on Sugriva's command. In a single bound they reached Kiskindha and gathered at the feet of their king. Rama and Lakshmana had been informed and came hurrying to hear the good news. Sugriva stretched and curled his tail in delight. It was a joyful occasion when Hanuman was able to make his report before Rama.

Afterwards Rama and Lakshmana took Hanuman along with them to their cave at Prasravana, where Rama was able to question Hanuman more closely and hear at length about Sita. Hanuman narrated everything. At the right moment in his story he produced the jewel entrusted to him by Sita. Rama pressed it to his heart with tears in his eyes.

'This jewel was given to Sita at her wedding by her father King Janaka. By seeing it I see Sita. Go on, tell me again and again whatever Sita said to you.'

Hanuman and his companions celebrate in the garden of Madhuvana by getting intoxicated through drinking wild honey.

'She begged you to act fast, for she cannot survive much longer. I offered to bring her to you on my back, there and then, but she said that it would not be right. She wanted you personally to come and defeat Ravana, then carry her back to Ayodhya in glory.'

Hanuman went on to deliver Sita's personal message to Rama about the time he had painted her face, and her final plea that he not waste a moment, for she would not survive more than a month.

'Take me to her at once,' cried Rama. 'Now that I know where she is I do not want to delay a moment longer.'

THE SIXTH BOOK

Yuddha Kanda

Rama and his army of monkeys find a way across the sea to Lanka and demand the return of Sita. Ravana refuses to surrender Sita, and a great confrontation between the monkeys and Ravana's demon forces is provoked. Here, the demon Malyavan tries unsuccessfully to dissuade the ten-headed Ravana from fighting with Rama, while Ravana's rakshasa generals wait impatiently for battle to commence.

RAMA VICTORIOUS

PREPARATIONS FOR WAR

ANUMAN, I CANNOT REPAY YOU,' said Rama, hugging him. 'I have nothing else to give than this embrace. Now we must consider how we are to cross the ocean, and this puzzles me.'

'There is no place now for doubt or sorrow,' said Sugriva. 'We must build a bridge to Lanka, then Ravana stands no chance against us. Transform you grief into anger, Rama, and nothing will stand in your way.'

'You are right, Sugriva,' agreed Rama. 'One way or another I will find a way across the sea, even if I have to dry it up. Tell me, Hanuman, of the fortifications of Lanka. How many gates are there and how strong is their garrison?'

'A high wall surrounds the city, though in places I have broken it down. It has four gates, each guarded by massive doors and catapults, and is surrounded by deep moats infested with alligators. The city is built on top of a steep mountain clothed in forests, and defended by millions of heavily armed warriors skilled in warfare.'

'Now the moon is in conjunction with Hasta,' said Rama. 'If our army departs this very day we will be sure of success.' He took command and through Sugriva issued orders to his generals. In excitement monkeys streamed out from the valleys and hills surrounding Kiskindha, assembling before their leaders. Soon a huge army set off south, spreading out like a tide. Day and night they marched, feasting on wild fruits and honey as they went. Rama rode on Hanuman's back and Lakshmana on Angada's. After several days they had their first sight of the sea, its foam-flecked surface reaching to the horizon and seeming to join the sky in a single limitless expanse.

They camped on the beach and Rama sat with Lakshmana as the sun sank to the horizon. His thoughts turned to Sita. What would she be doing at this moment? Perhaps the same breeze that blew from the sea had touched her.

'Sita is weak from fasting,' he said, 'and I fear that we may arrive too late. We must find a way to cross this ocean soon.' Lakshmana comforted Rama as the sun slid over the horizon.

Across the sea, Ravana sat late in his council chamber. Shifting uncomfortably, he reported to his ministers the extent of the damage done by Hanuman and asked their advice in the light of the reports coming in of a vast army of monkeys approaching the opposite shore.

'Rama will find a way to get across. How do you propose we defend ourselves?'

'Our armies stand at the ready,' one general boasted, 'so what have we to fear? We have crushed the whole universe, even the court of Indra, king of heaven. What do we fear from mere humans and monkeys?'

'Hanuman caught us unawares,' said another. 'This time it will be different. I will kill Rama and Lakshmana, and all the monkeys, on my own. The rest of you can stay here drinking wine without worry.' They brandished their swords but Vibhisana, Ravana's younger brother, restrained them.

'Rama is not so easily defeated,' he warned. 'It is dangerous to underestimate your enemy. Do you forget how he killed Khara? I advise that Sita be returned. That way we shall avert disaster.'

Disgusted at his brother's words, Ravana dismissed everyone and retired to his palace. But the following morning Vibhisana again sought Ravana.

'Brother, ever since you kidnapped Sita ill omens have been seen. Sacred fires are obscured by smoke, cows do not give milk, donkeys shed tears and crows cry from the roofs of the buildings. Everyone blames your sin of abducting Sita, but they dare not tell you. You must return her to Rama.'

'I am not afraid of Rama,' rejoined Ravana angrily, 'and I will never return Sita.'

Ravana had become a slave to his infatuation for Sita. The people of Lanka, even those close to him, openly disapproved of his behaviour, increasing his unease. Calling together his ministers and generals, he asked for their advice.

'As you know, I have kidnapped Sita, wife of Rama, and am passionately in love with her, though she is not yet inclined to share my bed. Now Rama is on his way with a great army of monkeys. We fear no monkey or human, yet I need your advice. How can we avoid returning Sita?'

First to speak was Kumbhakarna, the dangerous brother of Ravana, who slept six months at a time under the spell of Brahma, and had recently awoken.

'This act of kidnapping Sita was unworthy of you. You should have consulted us first. Nevertheless, I shall atone for your mistake by killing all your enemies. So rest at ease. You will not lose Sita.'

'Ravish her by force and have done with it!' interjected another demon, impatient with Ravana's infatuation.

'I cannot,' replied Ravana, 'because Brahma has cursed me that if ever I molest a woman against her will my head will burst into a hundred pieces. In fear of this I will not violate Sita. No matter. I will destroy Rama as I destroy all who oppose me.'

Vibhisana could no longer remain silent. 'Give up this folly. Sita is like a poisonous snake around your neck. Return her to Rama. Kumbhakarna cannot defeat Rama; he boasts because he has never actually faced him in battle, so he does not realize how powerful he is.'

'I have defeated Indra himself,' protested Indrajit, 'so why do you think I cannot defeat a mere prince of humans? You are a coward, frightening us for no good reason.'

'Child, you speak nonsense,' retorted Vibhisana. You are the enemy of your father because you counsel him to seek his own death, and yours too. No doubt death is what you both deserve, but you must give back Sita and let us live in peace.'

These words made Ravana furious. 'I would rather live with a snake than a supposed friend devoted to my enemy,' he roared. 'Although you are my brother you cannot be trusted because you scheme for your own self-interest.'

Vibhisana blazed with anger as he rose into the air and hovered above Ravana.

'I am your friend and servant, older brother, who does not wish to see you killed by Rama. However, you ignore my advice. Therefore protect yourself and your subjects as best you can. I am leaving you. I wish you well.' So saying, Vibhisana flew from Lanka in the direction of Rama.

A BRIDGE TO LANKA

Within an hour Vibhisana and four companions were over Rama's encampment, having flown across the sea. He called to Sugriva from the sky.

'I am Vibhisana, brother of Ravana. I come in peace to serve Rama.'

Sugriva sounded the alert, thinking them spies, and urged Rama to kill them. But Rama disagreed. Hanuman also was in favour of befriending Vibhisana, because he had saved his life.

'He has asked me for shelter. I am bound to give protection to all who surrender to me. That is my vow,' declared Rama.

Vibhisana descended from the air and fell at Rama's feet with his followers, pledging his allegiance. Rama asked him the strengths and weaknesses of the demons.

'Kumbhakarna, my older brother, is to be feared,' said Vibhisana. 'Indrajit can make himself invisible on the battlefield, which makes him invincible, and Ravana has routed the chief gods of heaven.' He described other leading demons and estimated their numbers at many millions.

'I know of Ravana's exploits,' responded Rama, 'but I do not fear him. I will not return to Ayodhya until I have killed him and all his followers. Then I shall install you as king of Lanka.'

'You can rely on my help,' assured Vibhisana. Rama embraced him and consecrated him there and then as king of Lanka before a crowd of monkeys on the beach. Then Rama withdrew to contemplate the problem of how to cross the ocean. He lay down on his side on the beach, resting his head on his arm, and gazed intently out to sea.

That night a spy sent by Ravana surveyed the beach encampments and hastened back.

'Their army is as vast as the ocean. It is time for you to take decisive action.' In fear Ravana sent Suka, a demon who could transform himself into a bird, as a winged messenger to Sugriva. The bird reached Sugriva's camp.

'Ravana sends his greetings with these words: "I have never harmed you, Sugriva. You are like a brother to me. Why do you oppose me? Go back to Kiskindha, for you will never conquer Lanka".' Monkeys seized the bird-demon to tear off its wings but Rama stopped them. He would not allow a messenger to be harmed.

'Tell Ravana that he is not my brother,' Sugriva told the bird. 'He is an enemy of Rama and therefore my enemy, and he deserves death. Lanka will be burned to ashes and Rama will slay him and his brother.'

Rama waited beside the ocean in deep concentration, determined that the Sea god would allow him passage or perish at his hands. Three days and nights passed but the sea god did not appear. Rama's eyes glowed red with anger.

'It seems this world respects anger, not patience. Therefore today I will split apart the ocean and dry up its waters, destroying all that live within it.' He took up his bow and released a flaming arrow that seared across the waves, threatening the lives of all aquatics and making the ocean boil. Rama fitted a second arrow to his bow. The skies darkened and the wind roared. Oceans, rivers and lakes trembled as the heavens thundered and lightning flashed. From the waters arose the figure of the Sea god, sparkling with gems and entwined by serpents, in the company of hosts of river gods. He spoke to Rama with joined hands.

'I will allow your monkeys passage. Tell the monkey named Nila, who was born of

Rama and his army cross their miraculous bridge to Lanka, supported by Vibhisana, brother to Ravana, who flies above them in the sky with his four companions.

125

the universal architect Visvakarma, to build upon my surface a causeway of rocks and trees and I will support it.' The Sea god then descended into the waves.

Rama summoned Nila and instructed him to supervise the construction of the bridge to Lanka. Work began and by the end of the first day the monkeys had progressed many miles out to sea, and the causeway held. After five days they completed the crossing to Lanka. The causeway was wide, straight and level and crossed the deeps as the Milky Way spans the skies. When all was complete Rama and Lakshmana, riding on the backs of Hanuman and Angada, led the army across. Monkeys leapt through the air or swam alongside them, roaring with excitement.

The great army assembled on the beaches of Lanka, finding ample provisions in the lush coastal forests as the sun sank in a crimson sky. Refreshed, they set off in the morning for the city of Lanka. Outside the city, Rama drew the army into the formation of a man, with Rishabha on its right arm, Gandamadana on its left, Sugriva at its legs, Jambavan at its waist, Nila at its heart and himself and Lakshmana at its head.

Suka the spy, terrified of being caught again, observed the crossing of the monkeys from the sky and flew back to Ravana.

'I delivered your message to Sugriva, but was nearly killed in the process. The monkeys are fierce and violent, but Rama protected me. He has already reached Lanka after bridging the ocean. The monkeys and bears with him number millions and are huge like mountains and clouds, covering the earth. Even now they are at the walls of the city. Restore Sita to Rama or be prepared to give battle immediately.'

'I will never return Sita. When Rama hears the music of my bow he will wish he had never come to Lanka.'

While Ravana sits in council of war, the demon spy Suka, after being released by Rama, flies back to warn Ravana of the approach of Rama's army.

Ravana sent two more demon spies to gather detailed information on the disposition of Rama's army. They left under cover of darkness and in disguise penetrated deep into enemy ranks, bewildered by the size of an army which spread from one horizon to the other and could not be measured. Vibhisana discovered them and brought them before Rama. In fear of their lives, they confessed to Rama that they had been sent as spies.

'I have no objection,' laughed Rama. 'Vibhisana will show you all you wish to know. Then you must go back and tell Ravana that tomorrow at dawn I will loose my anger upon him.' They were released and soon reported all this to Ravana.

'These four – Rama, Lakshmana, Sugriva and Vibhisana – can tear this city from its foundations,' they reported. 'Do not trifle with them, my lord. Return Sita without delay and sue for peace.'

'Even if the whole universe attacks me I will not return Sita,' stormed Ravana. 'Take me onto the battlements and show me this great army.' They climbed to the top of the highest tower and looked down upon Rama's troops, surging like the sea at the foot of Lanka's golden cliffs. Suka pointed out to Ravana the leading monkey warriors and described each of their strengths, estimating their numbers at many hundreds of thousands of millions. When he saw their strength Ravana was shaken.

'You should not have praised those brutes in front of me,' he snapped. 'What fools am I surrounded with? Be gone and do not return, both of you, and consider yourselves lucky to keep your lives.'

Ravana sent yet more spies, wanting every detail of Rama's movements. They too were captured and humiliated before being sent back to Ravana. He was now thoroughly alarmed but firmly set against surrender. He went deep into his palace, where he sent for the sorcerer Vidyujiva.

THE OBSTINACY OF RAVANA

In his deranged mind, Ravana thought he might persuade Sita to marry him if he could convince her that Rama was dead. So he asked Vidyujiva to conjure up a false image of Rama's head and a golden bow similar to Rama's. He entered the ashok grove, eager to see Sita's beautiful face, and found her beneath the surviving tree sitting on the bare ground with her head bent in sorrow.

'I bring you news of your husband,' Ravana began. 'He is dead. Now nothing stands in the way of your union with me. This is what happened: last night Rama camped with his army on the opposite shore. During the night Prahasta infiltrated their camp with soldiers armed with swords, javelins, spears, scimitars, axes, clubs and arrows, and slaughtered them. Rama was found asleep and beheaded. Vibhisana was taken captive, and Sugriva and Hanuman were killed. There is not a warrior left alive who has not fled in panic.'

When all is ready for battle, Malyavan, Ravana's grandfather-in-law, makes
a last attempt to persuade the demon king to make peace with Rama.

Ravana then produced the false head of Rama, covered in dust and blood, and placed it on the ground in front of Sita, and next to it the bow.

'Here is Rama's severed head and his once mighty bow. Now you will submit to me.'

Sita recognized the head as bearing all the distinctive marks of Rama: his noble brow, his lotus-like eyes and the distinctive jewel he wore in the knot of his hair. She threw herself on the ground.

'Now I have no reason to live, for I have seen my husband die before me. O Rama! Astrologers predicted that you would have a long life, but now it is cut short. Why don't you speak to me? This girl who you married in your youth has turned out to be the cause of your death. Kill me, Ravana. Do one worthy deed in your life and unite this wife with her husband.'

At this moment Ravana was interrupted by an urgent message from his generals calling for his presence, and hurried off. As soon as he had gone, a curious thing happened: Rama's head and bow vanished into thin air. This was not seen by Sita, but by her friend Sarama, the wife of Vibhisana, one of the demon attendants.

'Dear Sita,' she reassured, 'do not be distressed by what you saw. It was a wicked illusion created by Ravana. Rama is alive and well. I have heard that he has crossed the sea and is this very moment camped outside the city walls with all his forces. Lanka is full of preparations for war: squadrons march on the streets; weapons are polished, elephants decorated, horses yolked; everywhere is the sound of drums and the rattling of chariots. But they will be no match for Rama. Soon your husband will take the city and win you back. If you like I can make myself invisible by my magic art and take a message to him.'

'Dear friend, thank you for your words of encouragement,' replied Sita. 'If you want to make me happy, please find out what Ravana is planning to do with me, for I am mortally afraid that he will soon have me killed.' Sarama left, returning soon with news of Ravana.

'Ravana seeks advice from his ministers,' she reported, 'and all urge him to return you to Rama and make peace. But Ravana is determined to keep you, even if he dies in the attempt. Therefore it is certain that Rama will slay him soon.'

A demon called Malyavan, grandfather of Ravana's wife, tried to advise Ravana.

'A wise ruler does not fight one of greater strength, he makes peace. You should return Sita and make an alliance with Rama that will benefit everyone. The creator brought into this world two orders of beings: the divine and the demoniac. In the great struggle between them the divine has the upper hand, being defended by Lord Vishnu, until the wheel of time turns to Kali Yuga, the iron age, when demoniac forces take control. Until then, us demons are destined to be the losers. You are about to be vanquished by the gods, who are working through the monkeys born from them. Moreover, Rama is Vishnu himself in human form, and he has come to destroy you. Submit to him and bring us all good fortune.'

'I hear nothing you say,' protested Ravana angrily. 'Rama is a mere human being whose father has forsaken him and who relies upon monkeys. What have I to fear from such a wretch? I will kill him and Lakshmana within a few days.'

Hearing these foolish words Malyavan left Ravana to his fate. Ravana then posted his generals at the four gates of the city and prepared to defend Lanka. Satisfied that all was ready, he retired to his private apartments to be with his women.

THE BATTLE BEGINS

On the eve of battle, Rama called his generals together. They climbed to the summit of Mount Suvela, from where they could clearly see the city of Lanka and what was to be the field of battle. As the sun set in a red sky, they saw the battlements of the city lined with densely packed rows of demons. The full moon rose and they spent their last night before the battle on the mountain top.

In the morning they saw spread below them a landscape of groves, lawns and water-falls alive with the songs of birds. Above this was the peak of Trikuta, on which stood Lanka, floating like a golden cloud. Behind its fortified gates they saw Ravana's golden palace, its turrets touching the heavens. On the battlements of the northern gate they were excited to see Ravana himself wearing a blood-red robe. Sugriva bellowed with rage and leapt from the top of Mount Suvela onto the battlements in front of Ravana.

'Today I will kill you!' he cried, and snatched Ravana's crown.

'And I will separate your head from your body,' shouted Ravana.

In a moment the two were locked in combat, wrestling arm to arm, chest to chest and leg to leg. Each was expert in the art of wrestling and strove with equal intensity. As they struggled they fell from the ramparts to the foot of the walls, but still they fought on, crouching, leaping and pressing each other's bodies until they were smeared with blood and dust. Neither had the upper hand and Ravana was on the point of summoning his sorcery, when Sugriva leapt high into the sky and returned to the summit of Mount Suvela, where he was greeted with cheers.

Rama and Lakshmana led the monkey generals down from the mountain and advanced the troops to the walls of Lanka. Armed with trees and rocks the monkeys waited in excitement for battle to commence, setting up a noise like rolling thunder and engulfing the walls of the city. Before ordering the attack, Rama sent Angada with a last message for Ravana. He flew over the battlements into Ravana's presence.

'Rama sends you this message,' he announced. "The time of retribution for your sins has come. For too long you have terrorized the innocent. Now I will punish you. Keep up your courage and I will slay you on the battlefield, thus releasing you from your sins and sending you to heaven. Prepare to die." '

'Take this evil monkey and put him to death!' cursed Ravana. Four demons seized Angada, but he soared with them high into the air, then shook them off so that they crashed to the ground. Then he flew back to Rama.

Standing before the walls of Lanka, Rama thought of Sita and ordered battle to begin. Hoards of monkeys began scaling the walls, smashing the defences with their rocks and trees and beating down the mighty gates. Waves of demons in dazzling golden armour rushed out eager to give battle. They struck the monkeys with maces, axes and swords, and the monkeys struck them with trees and rocks or with their teeth and nails. The fighting was fierce enough to make your hair stand on end. As the day progressed one after another of the leading demons was vanquished, and the battlefield was covered with spears, arrows, shattered chariots and dead elephants.

Darkness fell but the fighting raged on. Rama's arrows shone like tongues of flame. As the night wore on Angada gained the upper hand in his fight with Indrajit, smashing his chariot and forcing him to flee. However, Indrajit made himself invisible and returned to the fight, invoking the weapon of Brahma which he had used before

Indrajit, the son of Ravana and his most feared warrior, flies unseen in the sky raining down magical snake-arrows which blind Rama and his army, rendering them powerless.

against Hanuman. Under the cloak of invisibility he rained down arrows on Rama and Lakshmana. These were no ordinary arrows. They were deadly serpents from the regions of darkness below the earth, transformed into arrows that bit deep into the vital organs of Rama and Lakshmana, binding them as if by cords of steel. Rama was powerless to defend himself against Indrajit's onslaught because he was unable to see where his enemy was. Before long the two brothers fell to the ground immobile. Indrajit intensified his attack, piercing them with more and more arrows until their entire bodies were covered with his shafts.

'Go now to the abode of death!' he shouted in rage. Rama and Lakshmana, trembling in the darkness with pain and weakness, lost consciousness. Indrajit, believing them to be dead, flew in triumph to Ravana.

As the night ended and light returned to the field, Sugriva, Vibhisana and others discovered the two princes, hardly breathing and unable to move, lying on a bed of arrows. Drawing around them in a protective cordon, they gave way to despair. Only Vibhisana was optimistic.

'Rama's lustre has not gone. He and Lakshmana do not have the appearance of dying men. Rama will recover.'

Indrajit went to Ravana and announced that Rama and Lakshmana were dead. Ravana was beside himself with joy and the demons celebrated as if the battle were over. Ravana ordered that Sita be taken aboard the Puspaka airplane and shown the dead princes. She was flown in the Puspaka over the battleground. With her went a demoness named Trijata, who was her friend. When Sita saw the inert bodies of Rama and Lakshmana covered with arrows amid the terrible carnage she was beside herself with grief, but Trijata encouraged her.

'These princes are not dead,' she deduced. 'Their bodies shine with a brilliance which is never seen in those about to die.' But Sita was inconsolable as she was carried back to the ashok grove.

Rama opened his eyes. He looked beside him and saw Lakshmana lying motionless. Thinking him dead, he felt deep despair.

'If Lakshmana dies my life is worthless. Perhaps I could find another Sita, but I could never replace a brother like Lakshmana. He always comforted me when I was depressed, now who will encourage me?' He turned to Sugriva and said, 'I thank you for your loyal service. You and your brave companions must now return across the sea to your homes. You have done all you can for me and I am well satisfied. I release you from all further obligation.'

Just then a mighty wind blew and lightning flashed in the sky. All at once there appeared the figure of Garuda, king of the birds and eagle-carrier of Vishnu. He shone like blazing fire and was hard to look upon. In an instant the snake-arrows that bound Rama and Lakshmana were released and the snakes fled in fear, for no snake can stand the presence of Garuda. Bending low, he wiped the faces of Rama and Lakshmana and stroked their bodies. As he did so their wounds healed and their skin shone bright and smooth. He raised them from the ground and embraced them.

'You have saved my life,' Rama said in wonder. 'Who are you?

'I am Garuda, your friend of old. I heard of your plight and hurried here. Don't be curious now about our friendship. Go and regain Sita, and when your quest is complete, you will know who I am.' He circled Rama, spread his wings, and soared into the sky. The monkeys roared in delight and beat upon their drums, ready once more to face the enemy.

KUMBHAKARNA SPREADS TERROR

Ravana heard the roar of the monkeys and learned that Rama and Lakshmana had both recovered. Renewing his attack, he sent Dhumraksha out from the western gate with a company of demons, riding on a golden chariot pulled by donkeys. A fierce fight ensued, during which many were slain on both sides. For a while Dhumraksha held the field, but he was soon dead, his limbs shattered beneath a huge rock hurled by Hanuman.

Next was Vajradamstra. He led his forces out from the southern gate, where he worked into the midst of the monkey army, striking terror into their hearts. But Angada hurled a mountain crag at him, smashing his chariot and throwing him to the ground, then cut off his head, sending the panic-stricken demons back inside the city.

Ravana now sent out the mighty Akampana with a horde of demons. Dust obscured the armies and the earth grew muddy with their blood. Akampana slew many monkeys then turned his onslaught on Hanuman, striking him with volleys of arrows. But Hanuman struck him on the head with a big tree and the demon lost his life.

Downcast at the news of Akampana's death, Ravana summoned Prahasta, his commander-in-chief.

Kumbhakarna, the giant and terrifying brother of the demon-king Ravana, is awoken from his deep slumber. Maddened by the smell of blood, he strides into battle.

*Atikaya, son of Ravana, follows his dead brothers onto the bloody
battlefield, but is soon slain by Lakshmana's arrows.*

'I urged you to return Sita and avoid this war,' protested Prahasta. 'Nevertheless I am ready to defend you with my life.'

He ascended his glorious chariot and sallied from the eastern gate with one-third of Lanka's forces. The slaughter that ensued was terrible, creating a sea of blood and broken limbs. Prahasta attacked Nila, covering him with arrows, but Nila broke Prahasta's bow with a tree trunk. The two heroes tore at each other's limbs until at last Nila broke a great rock over Prahasta's head, ending his life and routing his army.

Angry and dismayed at the death of Prahasta, Ravana decided he himself would have to fight. Effulgent with mystic power, he led an army of gigantic demons out from the gates. Fighting with his twenty arms he cleaved a path through the monkey army towards Hanuman.

'Remember me? I killed your son Aksa,' Hanuman taunted. 'You may be safe from gods and demons, but beware of monkeys!'

Incensed, Ravana dealt Hanuman a huge blow on his chest, knocking him to the

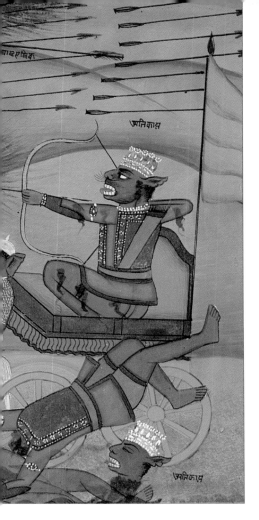

ground, and moved on. He then attacked Lakshmana and wounded him grievously with his javelin, but Hanuman knocked Ravana aside and carried Lakshmana to safety, where his wounds miraculously healed.

Rama then attacked Ravana, destroying his chariot and weapons, and striking him with a formidable arrow in his chest. In pain, the king of the demons dropped his bow and slumped to the ground. Rama spared him his life, allowing him to retreat into Lanka.

'Come back with a fresh chariot,' shouted Rama, 'and fight me again. Then you will discover my full strength.'

Defeated and disgraced, Ravana re-entered Lanka. He remembered Brahma's warning: 'Beware of humans'. He also remembered the curse of Vedavati, who foretold that she would come back as a woman in a future life and be the cause of his death. But he was not about to surrender.

'Wake Kumbhakarna!' he ordered.

Kumbhakarna, the brother of Ravana, was a monster who fed on flesh. Long ago when he was born he started eating all living beings at a frightening speed. To save them Brahma put him to sleep, allowing him to wake for only one day every six months. Ravana now ordered him to be awakened, although he had slept for only nine days.

Rakshasas descended into his underground mansion of gold, where his enormous form lay buried in sleep. They sounded bells and drums but he did not stir. They struck him with clubs and trampled on him, but still he slept soundly. Finally they brought hundreds of elephants to walk all over him, and at last he stirred. He yawned and stretched, calling for food, and they fed him on deer, buffalo and pigs with vats of blood and wine.

'Why have I been woken?' he growled. 'What danger faces Lanka?'

'The city is besieged. Rama has put Ravana to flight, leaving him only with his life.'

'I shall conquer him and drink his blood!' roared the monster. Leaping from his bed, he washed his face, and called for more drink. After drinking hundreds more barrels of wine he made his way full of excitement to his brother's palace. When he learned from Ravana the full extent of his troubles, he laughed.

'Did I not warn you, brother, that you were foolish to keep Sita? Now you are reaping the reward of your sinfulness and pride,' he chided. 'But never fear, I will put your enemies to flight and devour Rama.'

Ravana gave him a golden coat of mail and a huge golden pike. Maddened with the smell of blood, he strode into battle surrounded by an army of giant rakshasas. When the monkeys saw the colossal figure of Kumbhakarna step over Lanka's lofty battlements and advance towards them they fled in terror. With great difficulty Angada and Sugriva rallied them for the fight. Waves of monkeys attacked from all sides hurling trees, rocks and mountain peaks at him, but the monster felt no discomfort. He ploughed into their ranks, tossing them aside, trampling them underfoot, crushing them in his arms ten or twenty at a time and greedily thrusting them into his mouth until he was covered with their blood and gore.

Hanuman was the first to halt his progress. He struck him with a mountain peak so violently that the monster stumbled. But Kumbhakarna thrust his pike deep into Hanuman's chest, forcing him to retire, vomiting blood. Thousands of monkeys jumped on the demon and climbed all over him biting and scratching, but he threw them off or pushed them into his gaping mouth. Angada and Sugriva each attacked him with mountain peaks and Hanuman broke his pike. Lakshmana attacked him with arrows, piercing deep into his chest and hurting him severely. But Kumbhakarna wanted to fight Rama.

Finding Rama, he rushed at him in fury. Rama shot an arrow into his breast, making him bleed profusely. In delirium he ran amok, devouring all in his path, whether monkey, demon or bear.

'Here I am!' shouted Rama, 'ready to kill you.'

Laughing insanely, Kumbhakarna charged again at Rama, brandishing an iron club in his right hand. Rama released an arrow, powered by the Wind god, which severed Kumbhakarna's right arm. The demon lifted a tree in his other arm, but Rama severed that one too with another arrow, and with two more he cut off his feet. Still he advanced, flying through the air with his horrific mouth open like a gateway to hell. Rama took a golden arrow encrusted with diamonds and sent it blazing through the air. It tore off the demon's head and mercifully brought an end to Kumbhakarna's reign of terror. The earth shook, celestials gathered in the sky to applaud and the monkeys went wild with joy.

THE FALL OF INDRAJIT

The news of his brother's death came as a terrible blow to Ravana. Now he realized he had been wrong not to listen to Vibhisana's advice. Seeing his despair, his sons rallied around him.

'You can still defeat Rama,' they assured him. 'We will kill him ourselves.'

Ravana felt his old enthusiasm return. His sons were, after all, powerful fighters who could fly through the air and knew the magic arts. Together four of them went out. They were met by fierce fighting and soon the ground was covered with the blood

*Hanuman carrying a mountain peak of herbs
to Lanka. The herbs heal the wounded monkeys
and bears and bring the dead back to life.*

of the contestants. One by one, Ravana's sons were slain by the fury of the monkey-chiefs. Last to go was Atikaya, equal in might to Ravana. As he went forth on his chariot, brilliant as a thousand suns, the monkeys thought he was Kumbhakarna himself, come back to life.

Lakshmana challenged him but he laughed, 'You are a mere boy, I advise you to leave unless you want to die.'

Lakshmana, however, was more than a match for him. Atikaya was protected by Brahma, so only a weapon powered by Brahma could kill him. Lakshmana knew this and invoked Brahma's blessing on his arrow, which cut off Atikaya's head.

With all his sons, save Indrajit, killed in battle, Ravana at last recognized his opponent as Vishnu himself, from whom there could be no defence. But Indrajit would not allow him to give up the fight.

'You will see Rama and Lakshmana lying dead on the battlefield today, killed by my arrows,' he pledged.

Before going to fight, Indrajit offered oblations into the sacred fire. The Fire god rose dazzling from the flames to accept his offerings and gifted Indrajit with the cloak of invisibility, which allowed him to move unseen on the battlefield. He summoned his enchanted chariot, which flew through the air, and set off to do battle, accompanied by monsters riding animals such as tigers, scorpions, crows and serpents. This hideous assembly issued from the city gates, longing for victory over their tormentors.

Indrajit ranged the sky and began showering devastating arrows upon the leaders of Rama's army. Moving like lightning, always hidden from view, he left them helpless to defend themselves. His incessant barrage soon overpowered the monkey chiefs and even Rama and Lakshmana. When he saw that they had all fallen on the field of battle, Indrajit withdrew in exultation to the city of Lanka.

However, Vibhisana and Hanuman had survived Indrajit's onslaught. Roaming the scene of devastation Vibhisana discovered Jambavan, lying wounded on the ground. The venerable bear whispered to him.

'Does Hanuman live?'

'Yes,' answered Vibhisana, 'but why do you only enquire of Hanuman?'

'Because he has the power to save us all. In the northern marches of the Himalayas, between the lofty peaks of Kailasha and Rishabha, is a mountain thick with healing herbs. Among them are four herbs of unmatched potency: the herb which brings the dead to life, the herb which heals wounds, the herb which mends broken limbs and the herb which revitalizes the entire body. These rare herbs must be collected by Hanuman if we are to survive.'

Hanuman was soon coursing through the air on his way north. He passed over forests, cities, fertile plains and rivers and drew near to the mountain fastness of the Himalaya range, whose white peaks shone like clouds. Among them he found the mountain of herbs, just as Jambavan had said, and searched all over it for the precious medicines. Unable to find them he tore the summit from its roots and bore it away to Lanka. When he brought it to the battlefield, the fragrance of the herbs wafted over the wounded and healed their wounds. In addition, all those monkeys who had died in the battle were restored to life. The demons, however, had thrown all their dead into the ocean to conceal their numbers and hence none was saved.

When they came to know of the revival of the monkey army, other demon champions came forward to fight, but they all perished, killed by Sugriva, Hanuman and Rama. The monkeys' fighting spirit was high, while all looked bleak for the demons. Indrajit desperately thought how to discourage Rama and his army. If he could convince Rama that Sita was dead, surely Rama would give up in despair and Lanka would be saved. He used his sorcery to conjure up an illusory image of Sita, placed her on his chariot, and drove before the opposing army with a company of demons.

Hanuman hurls boulders at Indrajit, Ravana's son. Both were protected by Brahma the creator, who stands in the foreground.

Hanuman was astonished to see on Indrajit's chariot the figure of Sita. Her torn sari and pale, beautiful face were distinctly recognizable. But what was Indrajit doing with her? The demon took hold of her hair and dragged her towards him, beating her mercilessly. Hanuman was enraged. He surged forward with other monkeys intent on stopping Indrajit.

'You are pitiless and cruel. By this foul act you are sending yourself to hell!'

'I agree that this woman should not be killed,' taunted Indrajit, 'but sometimes such things must be done in war. Watch me as I kill this princess, so dear to Rama.' Hanuman looked on in horror as he raised his sharpened sword and with a single stroke clove her in two, spilling her blood in his chariot. Enraged, Hanuman flew at Indrajit and aimed a huge rock to crush him and his chariot. But Indrajit speedily withdrew, leaving his army to be decimated by the outraged monkeys.

Hanuman told Rama the ghastly news. When Rama heard it he fell to the ground like a fallen tree and went into a deep depression. Lakshmana hurried to comfort him. Bewildered by this unforeseen turn of events, the two brothers remained in a state of shocked disbelief until Vibhisana arrived on the scene. When he was told what had happened he knew straight away that this was a trick of Indrajit's. He patiently explained to Rama the truth.

'Ravana would never allow Sita to be killed – he is too attached to her. This is a trick of Indrajit's, who loves to use his sorcery to delude his opponents. Even now he is at the fire sanctuary preparing offerings for the Fire god. Twice already he has overcome us through occult means, and if he is allowed to complete one more such ritual, he will become invisible again and gain sufficient powers to defeat us for good. We must prevent him. Let me take Lakshmana to that place to finish Indrajit once and for all.' Rama gave his blessings and they hurried off.

On the way Vibhisana asked Hanuman to launch an attack on the demon army so as to force Indrajit to leave his sanctuary to fend them off. Hanuman led the onslaught, armed with rocks and trees, and before long they had put the demon army to flight. Sure enough, Indrajit appeared in rage to defend them.

While Hanuman did this Vibhisana and Lakshmana reached the place of sacrifice. Leading him through a dense thicket of ancient trees, Vibhisana brought Lakshmana to a clearing around a blackened banyan tree which spread its hoary branches over the fire sanctuary. Smoke rose from the fire-pit which was surrounded by ritual artifacts, and female attendants waited for Indrajit, who had evidently left in a hurry and was expected back. Suddenly Indrajit appeared, alerted by his aides of their presence in his inmost sanctuary. Deeply angered, he turned upon Vibhisana.

'You are Ravana's brother and my uncle, yet you have become our enemy, and now you have betrayed my secret. I despise you for this.'

'Although I was born a demon, that is not my nature,' replied Vibhisana. 'I have chosen a different path, driven away by the sinfulness of my family.'

Indrajit turned with contempt to Lakshmana.

'Have you come for more punishment? Do you forget that twice already I have crushed you? Stay then and fight, and I will fill you with arrows that will consume you as fire consumes a ball of cotton.' So saying, he loosed a volley of arrows that pierced Lakshmana through, hissing like serpents. Lakshmana replied with five steel shafts that penetrated deep into his chest. And so the duel went, each displaying dazzling skills and strength, and seemingly invulnerable to the other's arrows. They deployed cosmic weapons against each other until they had exhausted their arsenals. Gradually Indrajit, without the benefit of his invisibility, began to weaken in the face of Lakshmana's fury.

Lakshmana invoked the glorious weapon of Indra, awarded to him by Vishvamitra in his youth. He took the arrow, fretted with gold and guided by delicate feathers, and fitted it to his bow. Chanting mantras to Indra and invoking the name of Rama, he drew the arrow back to his ear, then released it. It flew straight and true and severed Indrajit's head from his shoulders.

The gods, watching from the sky, showered flowers on Lakshmana and praised his deed. Rama hugged him close, soothing his injured limbs and ridding him of all pain. With the help of the healing herbs he soon recovered from his ordeal. They all looked forward to the final showdown with Ravana.

THE END OF RAVANA

Ministers hastened to Ravana with the news of Indrajit's demise. Stunned, the lord of demons fell into a nerveless state, pondering his great loss. After some time he stirred, knitting his brows and grinding his teeth. He screamed, venting smoke and flames from his cavernous mouth, and seized his razor-edged sword, resolving to put an end to Sita, the cause of all his troubles. He swept out of his chambers, sending courtiers scurrying for shelter, and hurried down to the ashok grove, anxiously followed by his ministers and his wife Mandodari. Sita saw his purposeful approach and the long sword at his side and thought her life was at an end. Weak with fear and resignation, she bowed her head and waited. Suddenly an elderly minister, Suparsva, spoke up.

'Surely you will not do this heinous crime? Since childhood you have honoured your religion. Will you now destroy all your merits in one instant by murdering an innocent woman? Turn your anger on Rama, not on this helpless princess!'

Ravana heeded these words of his trusted adviser and withdrew his sword. With this friend of his he returned to his council chamber.

Ravana believed himself invulnerable. He had a coat given to him by Brahma that was impenetrable, even by the arrows of Indra. He therefore determined to kill Rama and Lakshmana himself. He ordered his remaining generals to gather whatever was left of his army – still an enormous force – and go ahead, with him following them to complete the task.

The great army advanced from the city, flying colourful banners and bristling with weapons. But this was not to be their day. Rama put on such a display of fighting power that even he was astonished. So fierce was his onslaught and so swift his progress, that the demons could not actually see him as he destroyed them. As one cannot see a hurricane flattening a forest, they could only see their warriors falling on all sides. At other times it seemed to them they saw not one but hundreds of Ramas. He became like the wheel of Time, bringing death to all who looked upon him. Within two hours, he exterminated the entire demon army with his fire-laden arrows, save a few who managed to escape.

Lanka was filled with the bitter tears of the demon's wives, sisters and daughters.

'We blame Surpanakha,' they cried. 'That ugly and deformed creature should never have touched the handsome Rama. Nor should Ravana have stolen Sita once he saw how easily Rama disposed of his cousins Khara and Dusana. Later the invincible demons Viradha and Kabandha, and even Vali the powerful monkey king were all effortlessly killed by Rama, but still this obstinate Ravana will not release Sita. Now he has caused the death of our husbands and brothers.'

Ravana heard their wailing and bit his lips in rage. Gathering the remnants of his once great army, and the few generals to have survived the morning's holocaust, he rode out to face Rama. His chariot was resplendent with jewelled pillars and golden domes, and equipped with a huge arsenal of celestial missiles. Rows of tiny bells jingled as it moved across the field, pulled by eight horses. But just then a vulture alighted on top of the chariot, other birds gave harsh cries, his left eye twitched and his face grew pale, while across the heavens flamed a meteor. Heedless of these omens, Ravana advanced to his doom.

The fighting went against him, and soon his generals were killed by Sugriva and Angada, leaving Ravana virtually alone. Full of rage, he invoked a spell in the name of Rahu, the planet of darkness that eclipses the moon, and cast it over the monkey army, destroying many of them. Then he turned his attention towards Rama, and the two of them entered a full-scale contest of arms. As they circled each other loosing thunderous missiles charged with mystic potencies, the sky darkened and all creatures felt oppressed with fear. Although each was pierced repeatedly by the other's shafts, neither felt pain.

Ravana believed himself invincible. This picture brings him into the present-day context by including in his arsenal a gun.

Ravana's arrows flew towards Rama, manifesting heads of lions, vultures, snakes and wolves with open jaws projecting sharpened teeth. Rama met them with arrows of fire appearing like suns, moons, meteors and comets.

Lakshmana and Vibhisana joined the attack, breaking Ravana's bow and killing his horses, forcing him to jump to the ground. Enraged, Ravana took up a javelin invested with deep magic, hung with eight bells and shining like fire, and launched it at Lakshmana with a sound like thunder. Rama, seeing it closing on Lakshmana, chanted mantras for his protection, but the javelin sank deep into Lakshmana's chest and felled him like a stone.

Rama rushed to Lakshmana's side fearing the worst, and with great difficulty extracted the shaft from his chest. But he showed no signs of life. Rama, his eyes full of tears, entrusted him to the care of Susena, the monkey physician, and swore that he would put an end to Ravana that very day.

When Susena saw Lakshmana's serious condition, he called for Hanuman to collect more precious herbs from the Himalayas. Hanuman again set off north for the mountain of herbs. Reaching there, he broke off a further crag from its summit and hastened back to the scene of the battle. Susena selected a herb called Visalyakarani, which has the power to expel from the body any weapon that has penetrated it and to heal the wound made by its entry. He crushed the herb and administered it through Lakshmana's nostrils, curing him instantly. Lakshmana stood up, all pain and injury gone, and was embraced by Rama and cheered by the monkeys.

The time for the final act of war had arrived: the destruction of Ravana. Indra, the king of heaven, decided it was time to give Rama some help. He summoned his trusted charioteer, Matali, and sent him and his chariot to Rama's assistance. All at once Indra's chariot swept down from the skies and halted before Rama, hovering in the air with its bells tinkling. Rama and Lakshmana recognized it as the same golden chariot, yolked to four green horses, that they had seen at Sarabhanga's ashram in the forest at the start of their exile. Matali greeted Rama and invited him to mount the chariot, holding Indra's shining armour and celestial weapons.

Rama mounted the chariot, which lit up the battlefield with its splendour, and set off in pursuit of Ravana. The combat was opened by Ravana, who released a demoniac missile which turned into thousands of snakes shooting fire from their mouths, assailing Rama from all directions at once. In reply Rama invoked the weapon of Garuda, the bird-carrier of Vishnu and enemy of all snakes, which produced thousands of golden eagles who devoured the snakes.

Ravana then raised another javelin, covered with spikes like mountain peaks and wreathed with fire and smoke around its point. It screamed through the air at Rama, threatening to destroy him and his entire army, but Rama countered it with a javelin of his own. When the two weapons collided the explosion illuminated the skies and showered fragments on the ground.

As the climax of the battle approaches, Ravana comes face to face with Rama, who pierces him repeatedly with deadly arrows. In the background monkeys hurl rocks and mountain peaks.

Rama shouted at Ravana, 'If I had been there when you stole Sita, I would surely have killed you then. But now that I do have you in my sight I will despatch you to the abode of death. Today vultures will feast on your heart and drag away your severed head as you lie shattered on the battlefield.'

The magical weapons Rama had received as a youth from Vishvamitra now came before him ready for his use, and Rama covered Ravana with arrows that bit deep into his body. The demon sank back in his chariot without the strength to fight on. Seeing this, his charioteer hastily retreated from the battlefield to give him time to recover.

While he was gone, the sage Agastya, who had been observing the fight from the skies, came to Rama's side. He recited in his ear the heart mantra in praise of the sun, which addresses the supreme God through the power of the sun, and allays all anxieties.

' "He alone creates, sustains and destroys all that lives",' he chanted, ' "He lives in the hearts of all beings, awake while they sleep, and is the supreme controller of all activities. All who remember him will be victorious".'

Hearing these divine words, Rama was rid of all fatigue and sorrow, and felt renewed vigour and determination. Soon Ravana's chariot returned with a sound of thunder and Rama took up Indra's bow to finish his task. Vultures circled around Ravana in a darkening sky, meteors coursed through the heavens, thunder rolled even without clouds, and blood rained down on his chariot. As the contest reached its climax, all warriors on the field, both monkeys and demons, stood motionless and watched in amazement. The denizens of heaven, observing from the sky, anxiously called out to Rama.

'May all be well with you. Delay no longer. Conquer this demon now.'

Rama fired a golden arrow which took the form of a serpent as it sped towards Ravana. It severed his head, but another head appeared on Ravana's shoulders. Again Rama cut it off and again it was replaced. Rama exhausted hundreds of arrows in this way, and the unceasing struggle passed through days and nights, neither gaining mastery over the other.

Seeing the situation, Rama's charioteer, Matali, advised him. 'The hour of Ravana's doom has come. To kill Ravana you must use the dreaded arrow of Brahma, given to you by Agastya, which never misses its target.'

Rama took out that arrow, in whose feathers resided the Wind god, in whose tip was the Sun god and the Fire god, whose shaft was made of ether and which was itself the essence of all elements. He charged it with its mystic mantra and dispatched it at Ravana with the speed of sound. Flaming and spitting, covered in smoke, it penetrated the heart of the king of the demons. Ravana's body fell lifeless to the ground.

All at once a breeze whipped up, dispersing the foul odours of the battlefield. The sky cleared and the sun shone with a warm glow. Flowers rained down and heavenly music echoed from the sky. Demons melted into the shadows while monkeys rejoiced and came forward to honour Rama, who was surrounded by his faithful friends on earth and glorified by celestial beings in the sky.

LANKA RESTORED

The battle was over. Ravana's huge body lay sprawled on the ground, covered in blood and surrounded by the gruesome aftermath of war, charred and mutilated remains covering the field as far as the eye could see. At his side knelt Vibhisana, with Rama standing behind him.

'O great hero,' mourned Vibhisana, 'why are you lying here, my brother, rather than on the sumptuous bed that you are used to? You did not take my advice. Now that you have fallen, the city of Lanka and all her people are reduced to ruin.'

'Do not lament,' said Rama. 'He terrorized the universe, even Indra himself. Sooner or later he had to die, and he chose to die the glorious death of a warrior.'

'He was generous to his friends and ruthless to his enemies,' said Vibhisana, 'and religious according to his own tradition – he chanted the Vedic hymns and kept a sacred fire burning in his home.'

'Now you must consider how to perform his funeral rites,' said Rama.

'He was my older brother, but he was also my enemy and lost my respect. He was cruel and deceitful, and violated other mens' wives. I do not know if he deserves a proper cremation,' confessed Vibhisana.

'He was immoral and untruthful, after the nature of a rakshasa,' replied Rama, 'but he was gifted and brave. Cremate him with respect and let enmity end with death.'

Then came Ravana's wives, braving the horrors of the battlefield to be at their husband's side. They threw themselves around him, sobbing and stroking his head.

'If only you had heeded Vibhisana and returned Sita to Rama,' they cried, 'none of this would have happened and we would be spared the curse of becoming widows.'

'How could you, who conquered heaven, be overcome by a man wandering in the forest?' spoke Mandodari, Ravana's chief queen. 'The only explanation is that Vishnu, the Great Spirit and eternal sustainer of the worlds, took human form as Rama to finish your life. Sita was the cause of your downfall. The moment you touched her your end was assured. The only reason the gods did not strike you down was because they feared you, but your actions still brought the fruits they deserved. One who does good gains happiness and the sinner reaps misery; no one can escape this law.

'You were advised by me, Maricha, Vibhisana, your brother Kumbhakarna, and my father, but you ignored us all.' Mandodari wept on Ravana's breast and her fellow wives tried to console her.

Meanwhile Rama sent Vibhisana into the ruined city of Lanka to make the funeral arrangements and perform the closing rites for Ravana's sacred fire. Soon he returned with the sacred embers, articles of worship and firewood for the pyre carried by rakshasha priests and attendants. They decorated Ravana's linen shroud with flowers and carried his body in procession to the beach, preceded by the sacred fires and followed by weeping rakshasa women.

Vibhisana ignited the pyre while the remaining family members threw rice grains into the flames. Vedic hymns were intoned as the mourners looked on in silence.

When all was finished they returned to the city. His anger exhausted, Rama put away his weapons. A deep joy welled in his heart and his gentle demeanour returned.

SITA'S ORDEAL BY FIRE

With Ravana out of the way, Rama's thoughts turned to Sita. He called Hanuman and asked him to take her the news of Ravana's death. He came to the ashok grove and found her as before, unwashed and uncared for with tears in her eyes, seated on the ground beneath the tree guarded by demon women. He stood respectfully at a distance to deliver his message.

'Lord Rama is safe and well, and has killed Ravana. He sends you this message: "After many sleepless months I have bridged the sea and fulfilled my vow to win you back. You now need have no fear as you are in the hands of Vibhisana, the new king of Lanka, who will soon come to see you". ' Sita was speechless with joy to hear this news and waited for more. But Hanuman remained silent.

'This news is more valuable than all the gold and jewels in the universe,' she laughed, 'and you have delivered it in such sweet words. I cannot repay you enough.'

'If you will permit me, I can deal swiftly with these cruel rakshasa women,' offered Hanuman, eager to be of service. 'They have so mistreated you. Let me kill them now with my bare hands.'

'You must not be angry with them,' reproved Sita. 'They have only done what they were ordered to do. Whatever I have suffered is due to my own sins, not to them. When others mistreat me, I will not mistreat them in return. I will show compassion to all, even if they are unrepentant murderers.' Hanuman checked himself.

'Then have you any message for your husband?' he asked.

'Tell him I long to see him!'

'You shall see him – this very day.' With these words Hanuman swiftly flew back to Rama with Sita's message, and urged him to go to her at once to end her misery. Rama sighed deeply in an effort to hold back his tears. After a moment he turned to Vibhisana.

'Go quickly and fetch Sita. Before bringing her here see that she is bathed, dressed in fresh clothes, and adorned as befits a queen.'

Sita waited in the grove, expecting Rama, but instead she saw the ladies of Vibhisana's household who came to bring her to his house, where Vibhisana told her to bathe and dress in preparation for meeting Rama.

'I want to see my husband now, as I am,' she protested, but Vibhisana prevailed on her to do Rama's bidding. The ladies helped her bathe and combed out her tangled hair, dressed her in fine clothes and ornaments and placed her inside a palanquin, covered so that no one could see her. Soon she was brought by a company of rakshasas to Rama's presence.'

During this time Rama remained deep in thought, considering how to welcome Sita. The strict codes of the royal house of Iksvaku demanded that a princess violated by an enemy must be rejected by her husband. Sita had been Ravana's prisoner for eleven months. Who knows what that immoral demon might have subjected her to? Rama trusted Sita completely, but he was determined that she must be publicly exonerated from any impropriety. He knew what he must do.

What happened next is painful to recount.

Monkeys and rakshasas crowded forward on all sides, anxious for a glimpse of the fabled princess. Vibhisana, hoping to protect Sita from the public, told her to wait in her palanquin, but Rama wanted her brought out in the open.

'These are my people and they want to see her,' he spoke sternly. 'At a time like this there are no secrets, even for royal princesses. Bring her here in front of everyone.'

Vibhisana was uncomfortable with this order, but dared not contradict him. Sita had to suffer the indignity of walking in front of thousands of curious eyes on her way to Rama. She reached him and stood at a respectful distance, her head bowed, and shyly looked into his face. As she gazed into his eyes her discomfort was forgotten for the moment and she glowed with happiness.

'I have won you back according to my vow,' announced Rama. 'The insult against me has been avenged, and its perpetrator repaid for his terrible offence against you. I am once more my own master. All this has been done with the help of Hanuman, Sugriva and Vibhisana, to whom I am indebted.'

Rama spoke without emotion, but his voice sounded strange as it rang out across the crowd. His heart bled for Sita, but he must not show it. She looked upon her lord, with tears falling down her cheeks, and dreaded what he might say next.

'I have redeemed my honour and won you back,' he went on, 'but I did not do this for your sake, fair princess, I did it for the sake of my honour and for the good name of the royal house of Iksvaku. Your honour is not so easy to redeem, since you have lived in the house of a demon who has embraced you in his arms and made you the object of his lust. You are so desirable, Ravana could not have resisted you for long. I

SACRIFICE

THE PRINCIPLE of sacrifice, called yajna, is central to Indian spirituality. Through it whatever a person takes from the world is returned and the earth, or the universe, is replenished. For example, clothes require cotton, therefore Gandhi spun daily with his spinning wheel; or when trees are taken to build a house, more trees must be planted for the future.

The symbol of this principle is the sacred fire ceremony, performed at weddings or festivals, or to celebrate a birth or a time of renewal. The sages in *Ramayana* performed the fire sacrifice every morning. The grains and cow's ghee poured into the fire symbolize that every activity – whatever is most precious – should be sacrificed for others or for God. The royal sacrifices conducted in *Ramayana* by Emperor Dasaratha and Rama honoured the devas as an extension of this principle. It is said:

"The devas, being pleased by sacrifices, will also please you, and thus, by cooperation between men and devas, prosperity will reign for all."

BHAGAVAD GITA 3.11

*Swearing her faithfulness to Rama, Sita decides to enter fire rather than bear
his insults. The Fire god, knowing her to be pure, saves her from harm.*

therefore relinquish my attachment to you. You are free to go wherever you please. If you like you can go with Lakshmana, or Bharata, or even Sugriva or the rakshasa Vibhisana. Do as you please.'

A shocked silence fell over the assembly. Sita tried to take in what she had just heard. She had never in her life received a cross word from her husband. Now he had condemned her in public with these awful words. For her this was worse than death. She bowed her head in shame before this crowd of strangers and cried uncontrollably as Rama waited in stern silence for her response. After a little while she wiped her eyes and stood straight, her face pale and her voice trembling.

'You speak hurtful words, my lord, as if I were a common prostitute, but I am not what you take me for. I am daughter of the earth, who was seized against my will by force. If you were to reject me it would have been better if you had told me through Hanuman when he first came. Then I would have put an end to my life and saved you the trouble of coming here to kill Ravana, endangering the lives of all these innocent people. You forget that when I was a child you took my hand and promised me your protection and that I have served you faithfully ever since. My heart has always remained fixed on you, but now you of all people do not trust me. What am I to do?' Sita's voice broke with emotion. She turned to speak to Lakshmana.

'I have no desire to live when I have been falsely accused and publicly rejected by my husband. Death is my only course. Prepare a pyre for me – I will enter the flames.'

Stunned at this request, Lakshmana looked at his brother. Rama nodded his assent. No one dared to contradict him, whose anger seemed capable of destroying the universe. Lakshmana mechanically went about his brother's bidding, and before long a funeral pyre had been built and set alight. The fire began to crackle. Sita circled around Rama in respect and proceeded towards the pyre. Standing before the blazing flames she called in a loud voice:

'May all the gods be my witness. I have never been unfaithful to Rama in thought, word or deed. If the Fire god knows me to be innocent, let him protect me from these flames.' Then she walked into the fire. As she entered the flames the crowd gasped in horror. The flames leapt high and parted over her head as she stepped among them, swallowing her golden form. For a moment she could be seen standing in the midst of the flames like a dazzling flame of gold, then she was lost to sight. Women screamed and fainted. A great cry, strange and terrible to hear, went up from all the monkeys, bears and rakshasas present. Rama sat immobile like one who has lost his life, and tears flooded his eyes.

As the incarnation of Vishnu, Rama had accomplished all the gods had asked of him. But the gods heard Sita's cry for help and were troubled at her ordeal. It was time for them to intervene. The creator Brahma, Shiva the destroyer, Indra the king of heaven, and others all boarded their aerial cars and flew down to earth, where they appeared shining in front of Rama and spoke to him.

'Have you forgotten who you are and who Sita is? You are the source of creation, the beginning, middle and end of all that exists. And yet you treat Sita as an ordinary fallen woman.'

'I am a human being. My name is Rama, son of Dasaratha, and Sita is my human wife. Who do you say I am?'

'You are the supreme Lord Vishnu and Sita is your eternal consort, the goddess Lakshmi,' declared Brahma. 'You are Krishna. You are the Cosmic Person, the source of all, creator of Indra and the gods, and the support of the entire creation. No one knows your origin or who you are, yet you know all living beings. You are worshipped in the form of the Vedic hymns and the mystic syllable om, and night and day are the opening and closing of your eyes.

'At our request you took human form to put an end to Ravana. Now you have accomplished this, and your devotees who praise you will be blessed for evermore.'

Then the Fire god, Agni, rose up out of the flames of the funeral pyre bearing Sita in his arms. She was unharmed by the fire and her clothes and ornaments, even the flowers decorating her hair, were exactly as before. Agni brought her to Rama.

'Here is your wife Sita who is without sin. She has never been unfaithful to you, in thought, word or deed. I command you to treat her gently.'

'This ordeal for Sita was necessary,' Rama explained, 'I had to absolve her from any blame and to preserve the good name of the Iksvaku race. I know she has always been faithful, but I had to prove her innocence. In truth I could not be separated from Sita any more than the sun can part from its own rays. But I thank you and accept, without reservation, your words of advice.' With these words, Sita and Rama were re-united. Then there was a further surprise.

'You have rid the world of the curse of Ravana,' said Lord Shiva. 'Now you have one thing more to do before you return to heaven. You must bring comfort to your mother and brothers and prosperity to Ayodhya. Greet your deceased father, whom I have brought from heaven to see you.'

Rama and Lakshmana bowed in wonder as Dasaratha descended in their midst, his celestial form shining. Reaching the ground he took them in his arms.

'I am so pleased for you, dear boy,' he said to Rama, 'and at what you have achieved. You have set my mind at rest, which has long been haunted by Kaikeyi's words, and you have redeemed my soul. I now recognize you to be the Supreme Person in the guise of my son. Now you have completed fourteen years in exile, please return to Ayodhya and take up the throne.'

Turning to Lakshmana, he said, 'Your service to Rama and Sita has brought Rama success, the world happiness, and will bring you its own reward. I am deeply pleased with you, my son.' Then he spoke to Sita.

'My daughter, please forgive Rama, who was inspired only by the highest motive. You have shown your purity and courage by entering the flames, and you will be revered henceforth as unequalled among chaste women.' With those words, Dasaratha ascended to heaven. It now remained for Indra to grant Rama one last wish.

'We are all pleased with your actions, Rama, and would like to grant you a boon. What is your wish?'

Rama was unhesitating. 'May all these monkeys and bears, who have sacrificed their lives for me, be brought back to life and returned to their wives and families.'

'It shall be done,' declared Indra. Then the monkeys and bears rose up, their limbs restored and their injuries healed, as if from a long and peaceful sleep.

'You may return to your homes,' pronounced the assembled gods. 'And Rama – be kind to the noble princess Sita. Make haste to Ayodhya, where your brother Bharata awaits you.' Then they boarded their golden aerial cars and departed for the heavens.

HOMECOMING

Vibhisana invited Rama to take his bath and put on royal robes and ornaments.

'I cannot bathe until I have been re-united with Bharata,' said Rama. 'For the last fourteen years he has lived as an ascetic for my sake. Now I must hurry to him. If you would please me, help me to get to Ayodhya as soon as possible.'

'That is easily done,' replied Vibhisana. 'The fabulous Puspaka airplane will fly you there by sunset. But first remain here a while and let me entertain you and your army.'

'I would not refuse you, Vibhisana, after you have done so much for me, but I long to see Bharata and my mother.'

Vibhisana summoned the airplane which arrived instantly, gleaming with its golden domes. Rama took the shy Sita in his arms and boarded the plane with Lakshmana.

'Settle peacefully in your kingdoms,' he told Sugriva, Vibhisana and their ministers. 'You have both served me well. I must return.' But they were not ready to part.

'Let us come to Ayodhya and see you crowned,' they protested. 'Only then will we return to our homes.' Rama happily agreed and invited them aboard with all their followers. Miraculously there was enough room aboard the airplane for everyone. When all was ready, the Puspaka ascended effortlessly into the sky amid great excitement. Rama took Sita to a balcony and they looked down at the island of Lanka.

'See, princess, the city of Lanka and outside it the bloody field of battle. Here, at Setubandha, is where we built the bridge across the sea and I received the blessings of Lord Shiva. Now you see Kiskindha, Sugriva's capital where I killed Vali.' As they approached Kiskindha, Sita made a request.

'Let me invite the wives of the monkeys to come with us to Ayodhya.' It was done. The airplane touched down and took aboard thousands before proceeding on its way.

'Now see Mount Rishyamukha, where I spent the rainy season in sorrow and where we first met Hanuman and Sugriva. And here is that enchanting place where we lived in our cottage and where you were carried away by Ravana, and over there is the place where the brave Jatayu died. Here are the ashrams of Agastya, Sutikishna and Sarabanga, and here is where you met the noble Anasuya, wife of Atri. Here is Chitrakoot, the most beautiful of hills, where Bharata found us.'

They stopped overnight at Bharadvaja's ashram and Rama sent Hanuman ahead with messages for Bharata. He was worried that Bharata might resent having to give up the kingdom to his brother. He need not have feared. Hanuman arrived at the village of Nandigram, outside Ayodhya, and found Bharata living as Rama had lived during his exile, dressed in deerskin, with Rama's wooden shoes occupying the central position in his court. When he heard of Rama's return he jumped for joy and hugged Hanuman, showering him with gifts.

The next morning Bharata led everyone out to meet Rama, with Rama's sandals at the head of the procession. A great cry went up when the people saw Lord Rama seated in the Puspaka airplane as it slowly descended. Rama came forward and took Bharata in his arms. Bharata hugged Lakshmana and greeted Sita, then he embraced one by one all the leading monkeys. Rama tearfully clasped the feet of his mother and offered his respects to the sage Vasistha. Bharata then placed his shoes back on his feet.

'I return to you your kingdom which I have held in trust for you,' said Bharata with emotion. 'By your grace all has flourished and my life is now fulfilled.' Again Rama hugged Bharata, while many of the monkeys, and even Vibhisana, shed a tear.

Rama was placed in the hands of barbers who shaved his beard and untangled his matted locks. Then he and Sita were bathed and dressed in royal finery. Sumantra brought up Rama's royal chariot and in grand procession entered Ayodhya, with Bharata at the reins and his brothers fanning him. Sugriva and the monkeys were welcomed into the heart of Ayodhya where Rama gave them the freedom of his royal palace and gardens.

For Rama's coronation, monkeys were sent by Sugriva to collect water from the four seas, east, south, west and north, and from five hundred rivers. Vasistha

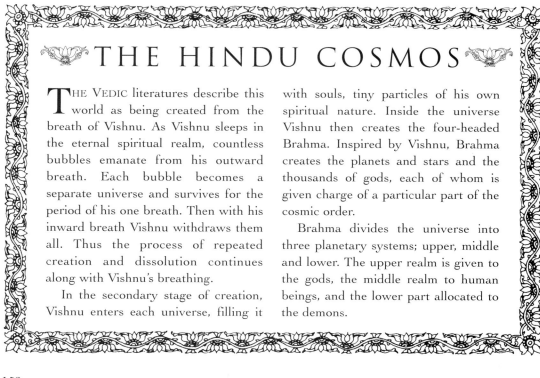

THE HINDU COSMOS

THE VEDIC literatures describe this world as being created from the breath of Vishnu. As Vishnu sleeps in the eternal spiritual realm, countless bubbles emanate from his outward breath. Each bubble becomes a separate universe and survives for the period of his one breath. Then with his inward breath Vishnu withdraws them all. Thus the process of repeated creation and dissolution continues along with Vishnu's breathing.

In the secondary stage of creation, Vishnu enters each universe, filling it with souls, tiny particles of his own spiritual nature. Inside the universe Vishnu then creates the four-headed Brahma. Inspired by Vishnu, Brahma creates the planets and stars and the thousands of gods, each of whom is given charge of a particular part of the cosmic order.

Brahma divides the universe into three planetary systems; upper, middle and lower. The upper realm is given to the gods, the middle realm to human beings, and the lower part allocated to the demons.

conducted the ceremony, bathing Rama with the sacred waters and installing Sita and Rama on the throne. Rama distributed gifts to all his people.

Sita looked kindly on Hanuman, unclasping her pearl necklace. She hesitated, looking shyly at her husband. Rama understood. 'Give it to the one who has pleased you best,' he said, and she placed it around Hanuman's neck.

During Rama's rule there was no hunger, crime or disease. People lived long, the earth was abundant, society prospered and all were dedicated to truth. For his people, Rama was everything and he ruled them for eleven thousand years.

Whoever daily hears this *Ramayana*, composed in ancient times by Valmiki, is freed from all sins. Those who hear without anger the tale of Rama's victory will overcome all difficulties and attain long life, and those away from home will be re-united with their loved ones. Rama is none other than the original Lord Vishnu, source of all the worlds, and Lakshmana is his eternal support.

Sita and Rama are enthroned on their return to Ayodhya, attended by Rama's brothers, by Vibhisana from Lanka, and by the monkeys and bears.

EPILOGUE

For many, the story of Rama ends with his reunion with Sita and his coronation as king of Ayodhya, yet there is more to the story. The seventh book of Ramayana, *called Uttara, or 'supreme', does not make easy telling, but I must tell it because without it my story will be incomplete.*

For a month after Rama's coronation, festivities and merry-making continued. When it was time for them to go, the monkeys cried and stammered; it was a sad parting. Last of all came Hanuman.

'My Lord, please grant my request,' submitted Hanuman. 'Let me always be devoted to you and no one else, and let me live as long as your story is remembered on earth.'

Rama hugged Hanuman and granted his wish, saying, 'Your fame and your life will last as long as my story is repeated, which will be until the end of the world.'

After Rama's guests had gone he spent many happy days roaming with Sita in the royal pleasure groves. In this way nearly two years passed. One day Sita appeared more beautiful than usual, and Rama knew that she was pregnant.

'My dearest Sita, you are going to have a child. Is there anything you wish?'

'I would dearly like to visit the ashrams across the Ganges, and stay one more night with those sages eating only roots and fruits.'

'Please rest tonight and tomorrow I will arrange it,' promised Rama.

That evening he sat as usual with his friends and chanced to ask them for the gossip among the people of Ayodhya concerning their king and queen.

'They praise you and your victory over Ravana,' came the reply.

'Do they say nothing against me?' Rama inquired. 'You may speak without fear.'

One of them admitted that men all over his kingdom spoke ill of his relationship with Sita. They said that since Rama had accepted Sita back after she had been touched by Ravana, they would now have to tolerate unfaithfulness from their own wives, because whatever the king does his subjects will follow. When he heard this Rama was astonished and turned to his other friends.

'Is this so?' he asked in dismay.

One by one they nodded, 'It is true, my lord.' Dumbfounded and full of grief, Rama dismissed them and sat deep in thought. After a while he sent for his three brothers. They arrived to find him crying. They bowed and waited for him to speak.

'In times of trouble you three are my life,' he began. 'Now I need your help and support more than ever.' He paused while they waited anxiously.

'I have just been informed that my Sita is not approved by the people – they think her unchaste. This is despite the trial I subjected her to in Lanka, where the gods themselves testified to her purity. I know her to be pure, yet dishonour, for a king, is worse than any other fault. I would rather die than fail to uphold honour.

'Therefore my mind is made up. Sita has told me she wants to visit the ashrams on the other side of the Ganges. Lakshmana, tomorrow you must take her there and leave her in the care of the sage Valmiki. Please don't try to dissuade me from this.' With a heavy heart, Rama took leave of his brothers and spent the night in sorrow.

In the morning Lakshmana set off with Sita in his chariot, driven by Sumantra, on the two-day journey to the Ganges. On the way Sita noticed strange symptoms.

'How is it, Lakshmana, that my right eye throbs and my limbs shiver? My heart beats faster as though I were distressed. Is all well?'

'All is well, my lady,' Lakshmana said. But when they reached the Ganges he sat down by the river and sobbed.

'Why are you crying, Lakshmana?' asked Sita. 'Do you miss Rama? Come, let us cross the Ganges now, and after one night we will return to see him.'

Lakshmana checked his tears and together they boarded a boat. Once they reached the other side and got out of the boat Lakshmana broke down.

'My heart is pierced by an arrow. I have been entrusted to carry out an awful deed for which I will be hated for ever. I would rather die!'

Sita was alarmed. 'What is it, Lakshmana? It seems you are not well, and neither was Rama when I said goodbye to him. Do tell me what is wrong.'

Sita takes refuge at the ashram of the sage Valmiki, the poet of Ramayana.

'Rama has heard unpleasant rumours,' Lakshmana stammered. 'It seems the people think you unchaste. In great pain he has ordered me to leave you here at Valmiki's ashram, although he knows you to be blameless. Valmiki was a close friend of our father and will care for you. Please stay here peacefully and hold Rama always in your heart.'

Sita fell unconscious on the ground.

'This body of mine was created only for sorrow,' she wept. 'What sin have I committed that I should be made to suffer like this? If I were not bearing Rama's child I would drown myself in the Ganges.

'Do as the king has ordered, Lakshmana,' she went on. 'Leave me here. Please wish my mothers well, and give this message to Rama: "You know I am pure, and will always remain devoted to you. To save you from dishonour I make this sacrifice. Please treat all your citizens as you would your brothers, and bear yourself with honour, then these false rumours will be disproved. You, my husband, are dearer to me than my life." Now look at me one last time, Lakshmana, and depart.'

'I will not look at your beauty now, lady, since all my life I have looked only on your feet,' said Lakshmana through his tears. He bowed his head at her feet and boarded the boat. Without looking back he urged the boatman on.

Sita remained crying by the riverside. Her cries were heard by the young ascetics of Valmiki's ashram and they brought the news to him. He gently brought her into his ashram, reassuring her that she need have no fear. Lakshmana, from across the river, saw her taken in and returned to Ayodhya.

Valmiki knew Sita was blameless and that she carried Rama's child. He took her to the women ascetics who lived nearby as his disciples, and instructed them to care for her as their own child. There Sita lived in peace and bore twin sons named Kusa and Lava. In time, Valmiki taught them his poem describing their father's deeds, *Ramayana*.

With help from Lakshmana, Rama learned to live with his sorrow after the loss of Sita, and found consolation in caring for his people. But he kept her always in his heart. Twelve years passed and Ayodhya prospered. To ensure the continued well-being of the kingdom, Rama decided to perform the exalted asvamedha ceremony, as had his father before his birth. When all was ready, the sage Valmiki arrived with Kusa and Lava and told them to recite *Ramayana* as he had taught them.

Kusa and Lava were asked to sing their tale for the king, and all present noticed their striking resemblance to Rama. After several days of recital the story revealed them to be the sons of Sita. When Rama understood this his heart troubled him. He sent word to Valmiki inviting him to bring Sita to Ayodhya, if she so agreed, to declare her chastity and exonerate her name.

Valmiki gave his approval and brought Sita to a great gathering in the presence of Rama. He stood in front of the people and spoke.

'Your majesty, Sita has lived under my care since you abandoned her. Now she has come to proclaim her honour. I, Valmiki, who never spoke a lie, declare these twin sons of hers to be your sons and Sita to be without sin.'

'Honourable sage,' said Rama, 'I have always known that Sita is pure and I acknowledge these two boys as my sons. The gods themselves vouched for Sita's purity. Nonetheless, the people did not trust her, therefore I sent her away, although I knew her to be sinless. I beg her forgiveness.'

Sita advanced into the middle of the assembly. In full view of all, with her eyes cast downwards, she made a vow.

'If I have always been faithful to Rama, in mind, word and deed, may Mother Earth embrace me. If I know only Rama as my worshipful lord, let her take me now.'

At that moment the Earth goddess rose from the earth on a beautiful throne. She took Sita in her arms and sat her on the throne, then withdrew with her into the earth. Petals fell from the sky and cries of adoration echoed from the gods.

Rama sank back in tears. He raged at the earth to return Sita, threatening to break down her mountains and overflood her surface. It was necessary for Brahma to appear before Rama and pacify him by reminding him that, as Vishnu, he would be reunited with Sita in heaven.

Rama mastered his grief. He returned to ruling his kingdom and caring for his people. In time, he installed his sons and his brother's sons as rulers. Eleven thousand years passed by.

One day a strange figure appeared at his door. It was Death personified, sent with a message from Brahma. The message said, 'You are the eternal Vishnu who sleeps on the causal ocean. In ancient times I, the creator, was born from you. In order to kill Ravana, you entered the world of humans and fixed your stay for eleven thousand years. That time is now complete. Please return to protect the gods.'

Rama set off for the banks of the Sarayu river, taking with him his brothers and all who were devoted to him. Ayodhya was without a living soul. Only Hanuman, Vibhisana and Jambavan remained on earth. Entering the waters of the Sarayu with his devoted followers, Rama left this world and returned to his eternal realm, where his devotees eternally serve the Lord of their hearts, forever reunited with his beloved Sita.

Rama welcomes his estranged twin sons Kusa and Lava to court. They sing the story of Ramayana.

GLOSSARY

ashok grove
Sita's place of captivity on Lanka, the isle of demons.

ashram
A hermitage, and also one of the four stages in life.

asvamedha
The horse sacrifice performed by Emperor Dasaratha in order to bear a son and heir.

atma
The individual soul.

avatar
Literally, 'to descend into': an incarnation

Ayodhya
An Indian city on the banks of the river Sarayu in the kingdom of Koshala, the seat of the Ishvaku dynasty ruled by emperor Dasaratha. The modern city of Ayodhya is in the northern state of Uttar Pradesh.

banyan tree
A sacred tree, often an object of veneration.

Bhagavad Gita
Meaning 'Song of God', the Bhagavad Gita is the essential text of Hindu teachings, spoken by Krishna.

brahmana
A priest or intellectual of the highest class.

Buddha
The ninth avatar of Vishnu.

Chaitra
The first of the twelve months of the Hindu year, equivalent of March to April.

Chitrakoot
A key stopping point in northern India on Rama's exile route on the way to Dandaka Forest.

Dandaka Forest
The place of Rama's exile with Sita and Lakshmana. A vast forest that once covered the whole of central India.

dharma
The essential purpose of life (see page 8).

Diwali
The festival celebrating the return of Rama and Sita to Ayodhya.

Ganges
The River Ganges crossed by Rama, Sita and Lakshmana during exile.

guru
A teacher and guide.

Iksvaku
The noble dynasty from which Rama descended.

karma
The law of action and reaction governing the movements of all beings, rewarding and punishing their good or bad behaviour (see pages 7, 52).

Kiskindha
Capital of the Vanara kingdom and the territory of Vali, the Lord of the Monkeys, in the region of Pampa.

kshatriya
A member of the ruling class of warriors (see page 99).

Lanka
The isle of demons and home of Ravana, equivalent to the modern Sri Lanka.

mantra
A sacred prayer or chant often used as an aid to meditation.

Pampa
The site of a beautiful lake on Rama's exile route in the northern part of the modern state of Karnataka

Panchavati
A forest near the river Godaveri close to modern Mumbai (Bombay), where Rama and Lakshmana first encounter the demons.

rakshasha
A demon.

rishi
A sacred sage. In Ramayana, rishis are often endowed with mystic powers.

Rishyamukha
The hilltop where Sugriva took refuge from his brother, Vali, in the region of Pampa.

sadhu
A holy man or woman.

samsara
The cycle of rebirth.

Siddha Aashram
The hermitage of the sage Vishvamitra.

sudra
A member of the working class (see page 99).

tapas
Penance, such as fasting, in order to achieve purification or mystic powers.

vaishya
A member of the class of farmers and merchants (see page 99).

vanara
A generic name for monkey.

varna
One of the four classes in traditional Hindu society.

Vedas
The original Sanskrit hymns that form the basis of all subsequent Hindu scriptures.

Vedic
The religious culture and tradition based on the Vedas.

Videha
The noble dynasty from which king Janaka descended.

ACKNOWLEDGEMENTS

To work on Ramayana has been a great privilege, and I am thankful for the opportunity, which came as an invitation from Channel Four and Collins and Brown on the eve of the fiftieth anniversary of Indian Independence. I am extremely grateful to Liz Dean of Collins and Brown for her professional advice and support through a very demanding programme of work. I think we all felt that by the end we had helped in the killing of Ravana and gained a little of the blessings of Rama.

NOTE
Great care has been taken to ensure the accuracy and authenticity of this text, which closely follows the original *Ramayana of Valmiki*. If any statement or implication gives offence, this is entirely unintentional.

PICTURE CREDITS
Illustrations on these pages appear by kind permission of the following:

Boston Museum of Fine Art 120, 126, 128.
Bridgeman Art Library (National Museum of India, New Delhi) 31, 62, 66, 67, 74, 78, (Private Collection) 134.
The British Library and India Office Collection, London 16, 21, 26, 27, 32, 39, 42, 49, 51, 58, 97, 100, 104, 116, 117, 118-119, 125, 138.
The British Museum, London 15, 19, 29, 113, 148.
Christies Images 2-3, 82, 94.
Freer Gallery of Art, Washington 20, 73, 108, 137, 155.
Ann and Bury Peerless 4, 65, 85, 89.
Werner Forman Archive 71, 86.
Victoria and Albert Museum, London 1, 22, 36, 47, 56, 75, 76, 81, 90-91, 95, 98, 110, 131, 133, 141, 143, 153, 157.

Front cover: Ann and Bury Peerless

First published in Great Britain in 1997
by Collins & Brown Ltd.
London House
Great Eastern Wharf
Parkgate Road
London SW11 4NQ
Published in association with Channel Four Television Corporation and based on the series produced for Channel Four Television Corporation by Sorab Irani of SBI Impresario Pvt Ltd., Bombay

Copyright © Collins & Brown Limited 1997
Text copyright © Ranchor Prime 1997

The right of Ranchor Prime to be identified as the author of this work has been asserted by them in accordance with the Copyright, Designs and Patents Act, 1988.

A CIP catalogue record of this book is available from the British Library

ISBN 1-85585-443-0

ISBN 1-85585-487-2 *(P.B)*

Editor: Liz Dean
Additional research: Lisa Balkwill
Designer: Alison Lee

Editorial Director: Sarah Hoggett
Art Director: Roger Bristow

Artwork: Amrit and Rabindra Kaur Singh, Twin Studio
Picture Research: Philippa Lewis
Cover design: Senate

Colour reproduction: Radstock Repro, Great Britain
Printed and bound in Singapore